A HISTORY OF WATCHET

WATCHET IN THE 1830's, FROM AN ENGRAVING BY J. W. M TURNER, R.A.

A HISTORY
OF WATCHET

By

A. L. WEDLAKE

THE EXMOOR PRESS

Dulverton . Somerset

© A. L. Wedlake 1973

This book was first published in 1955
by Cox, Sons & Co. Ltd., Williton. Revised by the author with additional
illustrations, and reprinted by The
Scolar Press Ltd., Menston (in collabor-
ation with Cox, Sons & Co. Ltd.), for
publication in 1973 by The Exmoor
Press, Dulverton, Somerset, England.

ISBN 0 900131 10 1

FOREWORD TO THE FIRST EDITION

It was in the late eighteenth century and early years of the nineteenth century that a leisured class of antiquarians, genealogists and historians set themselves the task of writing long county or regional histories ; they were followed by others whose work on town, parish or manor, if usually less ponderous, was only as authoritative as the integrity and capacity of the author permitted.

With the growth of county archaeological societies we find shorter but more detailed studies and papers devoted to prehistoric discovery, family history and particularly to the architectural merits of house, church and monastery. To-day the more comprehensive county survey is no longer the monopoly of the amateur historian, but has been taken over by university departments and by such bodies as the editorial committees of the Victoria County History, the Place-Name Society and the Royal Commission on Historical Monuments.

Yet the publication of the larger regional works has brought about a more general awakening of the interest in local and especially parochial history throughout the country, and this interest has been nurtured by such organizations as the W.E.A., the Women's Institute and the National Council for Social Services. There is, therefore, plenty of scope for the individual who, with roots deep in his native soil and an inquisitive turn of mind, can sort out, from an entanglement of fact, myth and surmise, a pattern in logical sequence of the story of prehistoric and early historic man in his own district.

This book provides both author and reader with the fulfilment of a desire : to seek out the rich background to a highly industrialized and often quite artificial existence to-day. Here we find a common meeting ground for practical archaeological fieldwork, enquiry into original source material, both written and oral, and a carefully balanced interpretation of the known facts. Where the evidence is lacking the writer plainly tells us so and uses what information he can obtain from nearby localities to paint in the missing shadows of his picture.

The story of the district is traced from the time when early prehistoric man came hunting wild game on the estuarine floor of the Severn valley, many thousands of years ago, to the commercial growth of the small township in the eighteenth and nineteenth centuries and to the economic position that Watchet holds to-day in West Somerset. The social life of its people, their misfortunes on the land and the obdurate battles with the sea to maintain their slender lifeline—the small harbour—are described succinctly and without prejudice. The author shows how when one project, which had brought a measure of prosperity to the townsfolk, failed, another usually took its place and helped to restore a balance of trade. In this way he brings out the independent spirit of the West Country folk and the conditions under which they have worked, played and worshipped through the ages.

This little West Somerset town boasts no important dramatic episode of national history. No engagements or battles were fought here, or at least not since the fierce encounters of Saxon and Viking, and few if any famous men have distinguished it by their birth. Poets and painters

may have rendered immortal some part of its quaintness
or charm :

> ' The ship was cheered, the harbour cleared,
>   Merrily did we drop
> Below the kirk, below the hill,
>   Below the lighthouse top '

wrote the poet Coleridge, but never before has anyone
thought it worthy of a book entirely to itself.

Visitors to Watchet will have been struck by the many
attractive features of the older town and harbour and by
the rocky coast which flanks it on either side. My own
earliest memories are cherished ones, for on three occasions,
as a small boy, my father took our family camping on an
Exmoor farm above Porlock, and the joys and beauty of
West Somerset crystallized as the little train from Taunton
to Minehead wound its way down the valley between the
Quantock and the Brendon Hills, and I caught my first
glimpse of the sea at Watchet station.

When later I came to live at Taunton Castle I took
my own family to visit and enjoy this stretch of charming
coast ; here it was, under the able guidance of my friend,
Leslie Wedlake, that my elder son and I were able to learn
something of the story of the town and harbour and to share
in the discovery of prehistoric remains of man and mammoth
in the gravelly foreshore at Doniford and on the cliffs and
hills of the district around.

Others I hope will enjoy reading the book as much as
I have done and appreciate the many hours of study and
research that have gone into its making.

WILFRED A. SEABY.

Belfast, 1954.

FOREWORD TO THE SECOND EDITION

Leslie Wedlake's admirable *History of Watchet,* first published in 1955, went out of print leaving a large and unsatisfied demand for it. The interval between that time and the book's re-issue has meant a long wait for the many people anxious to secure a copy, and I have been in a position to know something about the extent of the demand and the hope that eventually it could be met.

As Wilfred Seaby remarked in his foreword to the original edition, the author thought the little town of Watchet worthy of having a book entirely to itself. Demand has shown this view to be shared by many. They number natives, exiles, and people who have spent holidays in the town and savoured its character. All, perhaps, share a common ground of admiration for a town with a strong, independent spirit that has shouldered financial burdens arising from the harbour disaster at the beginning of the century.

The re-issue of this book coincides with local government changes that may tend to blur Watchet's form as an independent entity, but, thanks to Leslie Wedlake's story of the centuries, Watchet goes into the record . . . as itself.

JACK HURLEY.

Williton, 1973.

CONTENTS

ILLUSTRATIONS

AUTHOR'S PREFACE

DURING THE past few years I have derived a great deal of pleasure in digging out (literally and metaphorically) Watchet's past from the many and varied sources in which it has long been buried. On several occasions information has been rescued in the nick of time, while in one instance valuable historical records that I have handled within the past twenty or thirty years have, unfortunately, been lost or destroyed. One of my chief reasons, therefore, for writing this book was to preserve as far as possible the available information concerning Watchet and to set it down in such a form as to make a history of our ancient town.

In my opinion many local histories tend to devote too much space to the ramifications of local landowning families. Family records and documents are of the utmost value and importance to the local historian ; in this book, however, I have tried to preserve a balance between such sources and the records, regrettably all too infrequent, that give us information concerning the social conditions of the ordinary people.

One of the most difficult problems in writing a history of this nature is that of the ordering of the material. Strict chronological order is incompatible with a plan based on the logical interconnections of the subjects. In this book I have tried to present an overall historical story that advances in time from chapter to chapter ; and which can be read as a reasonably continuous narrative ; equally, the reader who is interested in one subject should have little difficulty in finding his material within each chapter.

My thanks are due to many friends, unfortunately too numerous for all to be mentioned individually, who have given me access to material and have so generously helped me in my researches   My especial thanks are due to Mr. H. W. Kille, of Minehead, for his invaluable co-operation and for the readiness with which he placed his considerable store of local material at my disposal ; and to Mr. Wilfred Seaby, F.S.A., lately curator of Taunton Castle Museum and now director of the Belfast Museum and Art Gallery, for reading the manuscript and making many valuable suggestions and for contributing a foreword. I should also like to thank Mr. R. C. Sansome, F.S.A., Scot., the curator of Taunton Castle Museum, for the loan of the plate depicting coins made at the Watchet Mint ; a plate taken from a photograph prepared for me by the Department of Coins and Medals, British Museum, some years ago. I am also grateful to Mr. F. N. Cox and members of the staff of Messrs, Cox, Sons & Co., Ltd., who have shown great interest in and co-operated so successfully in the production of this book ; and to Mr. T. E. L. Eley for his generous editorial assistance and his numerous and useful suggestions.

Finally I should like to pay a tribute to my old friend, a devotee of Watchet, Mr. J. L. Hobbs, of Barrow-in-Furness ; for on looking back I feel certain that his encouragement in the early stages of my researches was as important a factor as any in the creation of this book.

NINE ELMS, WATCHET.
MARCH, 1955.

Thanks to the co-operation of the Exmoor Press, the demand for the reprinting of this book has been satisfied. I am also grateful to Mr. H. H. Hole, of Williton, for supplying additional photographs, and Mr. Maurice Chidgey and members of the staff of Cox, Sons & Co. Ltd., Williton, for assistance.

NINE ELMS, WATCHET.
APRIL, 1973.

CHAPTER ONE

THE ORIGINS OF WATCHET

Geology

WE SEE LOOKING down from Cleeve Hill, which rises to the west of Watchet, or from the cliff lying to the east of the harbour, that the old part of the town nestles snugly at the mouth of a narrow valley. Many ancient towns and ports owe their existence to their immediate physiographical position, and I think there is little doubt that the ancient port of Watchet came into being as a result of such natural conditions.

We should have to go back many millions of years and unravel several complex geological problems to get a complete picture of the original formation of the valley. For our purpose it will be sufficient to start from the period of the Ice Ages, known to geologists as the Pleistocene period, and only mention the older rock formations as they affect the landscape.

During the past half-million years a large part of Britain and the Continent was on several occasions buried beneath huge glaciers ; these covered the northern and central areas of Britain from a line roughly stretching from South Wales to East Anglia. Below this line, while there are no traces of glaciers, we must assume that there were heavy snowfalls and that the ground was frozen to a depth of many feet. In short, conditions were similar to those obtaining to-day on the fringes of the polar ice sheets in Greenland and Spitzbergen.

There were four major cold spells or glaciations during this period, between each of which warmer conditions occurred ; the milder phases are known as interglacial periods, and it was during these times that valleys such as our own were the beds of quite sizeable rivers carrying the melting flood waters along with any loose material and debris to the sea.

The last time that floods occurred in our valley was at the end of the fourth and final glaciation, which is estimated to have taken place about 14000 to 12000 B.C. The Washford River, which runs out on the western side of the harbour, is the puny descendant of a once much larger river which was then as wide as the Thames is at Westminster to-day. To the east and west of the harbour are fairly high cliffs of Keuper Marl, a formation of the much earlier Triassic Age. These cliffs hemmed in the old river-bed, and as the floodwaters subsided the gravels were laid down between the cliffs, thus forming a level floor which runs inland and on which the old part of the town is now situated. Later, when climatic conditions became similar to those we know to-day, the softer gravel bed was subject to sea erosion at a much faster rate than the cliffs on either side, thus forming a cove or natural harbour. This harbour was on a coast which is naturally very open and rocky and must have been an ideal site for human settlement.

Beyond the Marl cliffs, at Helwell Bay to the east and Cleeve Hill to the west, the Triassic rocks dip and are covered by later rocks named the Jurassic, which are divided into the Rhaetic and Lower Lias. Fossils of various kinds of marine animals, fish, and reptiles have been found in these Jurassic rocks and for many years they have been a source of interest to geologists, palaeontologists, and other observers. As long ago as 1724 Daniel Defoe wrote : ' Walking on the shore at Watchet, I discovered among the large gravel great numbers of stones, fluted in imitation of the shells of fishes of all kinds. Many of the flat kind are double, and curiously tallied one in another, which may by a violent stroke be separated. How to account for the vast variety to be found here of this sport of nature I know not. Some I have seen as broad as a pewter dish, and again others no bigger than a pepper-corn, but in all of them the flutings are regular, some like the escalop, in rays from a centre, others like the periwinkle, in spiral lines, in these and other forms, they lie here in great plenty.'

It must be remembered that when Defoe was writing the science of geology was almost unknown and it was not until nearly a century later that William Smith, who has been called the father of English geology, began publishing the results of his researches. Half a century later Sir William Boyd Dawkins, a well-known archaeologist and palaeontologist, published some results of his discoveries in the Rhaetic beds of Watchet. His important finds included remains of fossil fish, the bones of a *pterodactyl* (a huge bat-like reptile), and the tooth of what was regarded at that time as being the earliest example of a British mammal. In the County Museum at Taunton Castle there are a number of good specimens of fossil reptiles which have been taken from the Watchet rocks. Among them is a fine example of an *Ichthyosaurus*, also that of a *Plesiosaurus* measuring twelve feet in length, both of which were large marine reptiles which have been extinct for many millions of years. There is also an excellent specimen of a fossil fish *Dapedius sp.* found at Watchet. Along the shore, either in the Doniford or Blue Anchor direction, will be found many of the fossil forms in the rocks, the Ammonites being especially plentiful. More careful search often reveals rare and unusual varieties : the writer has recently discovered good examples of fossilized wood ; a large portion of a fish, showing the scales and fins ; as well as numerous shell-fish of the Jurassic period.

Interesting fossil remains of a more recent age have also come to light in the neighbourhood : those of the

Mammoth (*Elephas primigenius*). These great hairy elephants
roamed over the southern part of Britain and the Continent
of Europe from the early part of the last Ice Age, somewhere
around 100,000 years ago. The earliest reference that the
writer has traced of mammoth remains being found in the
district comes from the *Taunton Courier*, March 1827, which
reads : ' A day or two ago one of the inmates of the Williton
Workhouse, whilst digging on the sea-beach near Doniford
came across the molar tooth of an elephant. The animal
must have been a large one, for the tooth, which is perfect,
is nearly a foot in length and weighs about a dozen pounds.'
We have also read that many years ago, when Watchet
harbour was being cleared and deepened, probably during
the reconstruction of 1861, two tusks of a mammoth were
found. In the succeeding years several tusks and teeth
were found on the foreshores at Kilve, East Quantoxhead,
and Doniford. All of these appear to have been found
casually on the beaches or foreshore. It was not until a
tooth was discovered by the writer *in situ* in the cliff gravels
at Doniford during the summer of 1949 that the definite
provenance of these mammoth remains could be established.
This has since been substantiated by the further discovery
of a large portion of a tusk in the lower gravel of the Doniford
valley in the summer of 1950. Such evidence gives us
definite proof that these remains were brought down by
the floodwaters during one of the interglacial periods.

While the mammals, fishes, and reptiles now fossilized
in the Lias lived millions of years before either man or the
higher mammals had evolved (e.g., geologists estimate the
approximate date of the Jurassic period, when the Lias
was formed, to be 150 million years ago), the mammoth
was contemporary with palaeolithic man. Ample proof of
this comes from the life-like drawings and engravings of
these animals (with others of the period) in caves in France

and Spain, which have been found together with the bones
of these creatures and the stone implements of early man.

Prehistory

Most of the material remains of primitive man that
we have are his stone implements, which were chiefly made
from flint or chert : materials which are very suitable for
tool-making and are almost indestructible. It is also known
that bone and wood were used, but the chances of finding
implements in either of these materials after such a great
lapse of time are very few. In Britain most of the palaeolithic (Old Stone Age) implements come from gravel deposits
where they were washed from habitation sites on the hills
and river banks by the floodwaters of interglacial times.
Several of these flint and chert implements have been found
in Somerset, where they occur in the area from the mouth
of the River Avon to the Blackdown Hills. Some of the
finest examples of the hand-axes, as they are called, have
been found in the river gravels of the rivers Axe, Otter,
and Yarty, and a good selection can be seen in the County
Museum at Taunton Castle. Very few have been found in
the past in the Watchet district. A rough chert axe, now
at Taunton, was picked up about sixty years ago on the
Quantocks above St. Audries, and during the winter of
1913–14 the late Mr. C. W. K. Wallis, of Birmingham, also
found several implements at Doniford. Among these was
a fine specimen of an Acheulian type of axe, now in the
writer's possession, Fig. 1, No. 1. Since then other examples
have come to light, one of which is illustrated in Fig. 1,
No. 2, but, on the whole, the implements of Palaeolithic
man are not plentiful.

The people of the Old Stone Age were hunters and
food-gatherers. They had no knowledge of agriculture or
the domestication of animals, but lived in small groups
and hunted animals over wide areas during interglacial

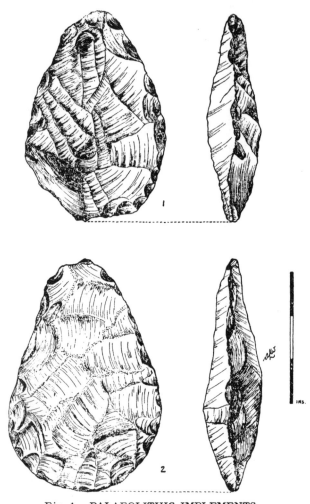

Fig. 1. PALAEOLITHIC IMPLEMENTS
1. Palaeolithic hand-axe found by Mr. C. W. K. Wallis at
Doniford in 1911.
2. Palaeolithic hand-axe found by the author, Doniford foreshore, 1953.

times. With these implements as evidence of Pleistocene or Palaeolithic man in our immediate locality, it needs little imagination to picture him, wandering over the ground on which Watchet now stands, in search of game.

Geographically Britain was vastly different then from what it is to-day. Instead of being an island it was joined to the Continent, and where the North Sea now rolls a great lowland plain linked Britain with Scandinavia. A land-bridge connected Britain to France in the south and to the west the land continued to Brittany, Spain, and Ireland. The Bristol Channel was a broad valley with the Greater Severn flowing through the middle. As the ice gradually retreated north and warmer conditions set in this well-watered valley probably became a main route for the large herds of animals moving up from the south in search of rich pastures.

It seems likely it was under such conditions that Upper Palaeolithic hunters came into the south-west after the final glaciation, which is estimated to have occurred somewhere between 12000 to 10000 B.C. This was the last phase of the Old Stone Age and it is noted for its varied and improved techniques in the manufacture of stone implements. We now have much more evidence of the occupation of primitive man in Somerset and the Bristol Channel area by late palaeolithic times. In the caves of Mendip and South Wales many examples of flint and chert implements have been discovered and collections of them can be seen in the museums of Taunton, Bristol, Wells, and Cardiff. The writer has a number of implements, probably of this period, in his collection ; some have been found in the Doniford area ; others come from Cleeve Hill and show features of great similarity to some of those found in the Paviland Cave on the Gower Peninsula.

A most interesting fact is that in the various caves of South Wales bones of almost all the species of animals found

in the Mendip caves have also been discovered. In one of
the former, Long Hole, remains of rhinoceros, bear, lion,
hyaena, bison, and reindeer were found; in another, Boscoe's
Den, 750 antlers of reindeer were collected. All these animals
are represented in the bones from Cheddar, Wookey Hole,
and other Mendip caves.

The Upper Palaeolithic age was short lived compared
with the older Lower Palaeolithic which had lasted at least
several hundred thousand years. Changes were taking place
rapidly, especially in climate, and conditions were becoming
generally warmer and more humid. Previously the vegeta-
tion was that of open steppe country, but with the changing
conditions forests and swamps gradually altered the appearance of the country. This was not a local change, but was
taking place all over Europe, and in consequence was having
an effect on the animal life of the period. Many of the larger
animals hunted by palaeolithic man had migrated to more
suitable surroundings, leaving only those animals that could
more readily adapt themselves to forest surroundings.

Somewhere around 7000 to 6000 B.C. new people were
wandering into Britain (which still had a land connexion
with the Continent), invaders who had evolved a new tool-
making technique; and it is thought probable that they
may have mingled with the people already living here. This
particular period of prehistory is named the Mesolithic
(Middle Stone Age), and we have abundant evidence of
Mesolithic occupation sites from the Quantocks to Exmoor.
Many hundreds of Mesolithic flint and chert implements of
this period have been found, a number of them being
illustrated in Fig. 2.

An important characteristic of the implements is that
for the most part they are smaller than those of the preceding
periods, so much so that in the past archaeologists referred
to them as ' pygmy flints ', while to-day they are known as

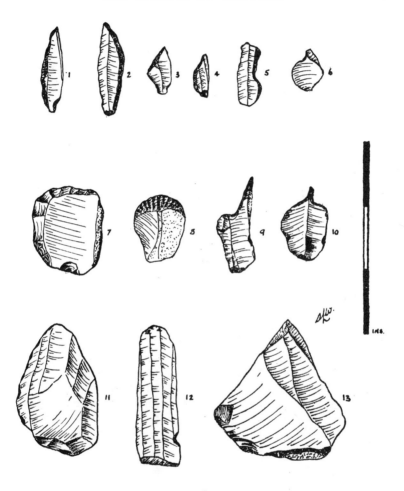

Fig. 2. MESOLITHIC IMPLEMENTS

1, 2, 3, 4. Microliths (Doniford).
5. Unfinished microlith (Cleeve Hill).
6. Micro-burin (Cleeve Hill).
7. Scraper (Cleeve Hill).
8. Scraper (Doniford).

9. Awl (Cleeve Hill).
10. Awl (Doniford).
11. Flake knife (Cleeve Hill).
12. Blade knife (Doniford).
13. Angle graver (Doniford).

microliths.   They are extremely small blades of flint or
chert with the back, or thicker part of the flake, carefully
blunted, Fig. 2, Nos. 1-5.   It is difficult to imagine how some
were used as they are so minute, but it is now known that
certain forms were inserted in grooves on the sides of bone
and wooden points, thus they could have been used as barbs
on harpoons, spears, or even arrow shafts.   Several bone
points [harpoons?] have been found on Continental sites
with the flint microliths still in position.   Opposite, on the
coast of South Wales, Mesolithic sites have also been discovered and comparison with the implements from the
Watchet district shows similarities both in form and material.
It suggests a close contact with South Wales at this period,
just as there was in previous and later ages.

There seems every reason to believe that for a period,
perhaps of three or four thousand years, these people at
intervals, probably regulated by climate or season, inhabited
our district, wandering over the countryside and across the
broad valley that is now the Bristol Channel, to Wales,
hunting game and gathering nuts, berries and other articles
of food.   Fishing, too, is known to have had an important
place in their economy and the shores of the Severn, which
flowed through the valley, were probably much visited.
Mr. F. J. North, in his book, *The Evolution of the Bristol
Channel*, suggests that about this time the estuary of the
River Severn was below Minehead.   This estuary would
probably have been a good collecting ground for shell-fish
of all kinds and it is worth noting that, on a number of the
habitation sites where implements have been found, oyster
shells are quite common.

The Stone Age was now nearing its close : the last
phase named the Neolithic or New Stone Age took place in
Britain as a result of fresh invasions from the Continent
somewhere around 2500 B.C.   This period meant a complete

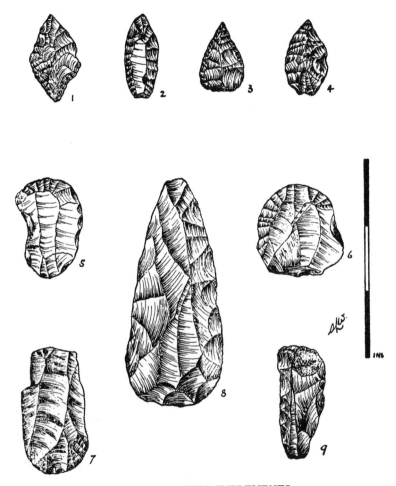

Fig. 3.   NEOLITHIC IMPLEMENTS

1, 2.   Leaf-shaped arrow-heads (Nine Elms
          Nursery, Watchet).
3.   Leaf-shaped arrow-head (Doniford).
4.   Leaf-shaped arrow-head (Cleeve Hill).

5.   Scraper (Doniford).
6.   Scraper (Cleeve Hill).
7.   Core hammer (Doniford).
8.   Unpolished axe (Doniford).
9.   Punch (Doniford).

revolution in the economy of primitive man. Throughout
the Palaeolithic and Mesolithic periods men had simply been
hunters and food-gatherers, but the Neolithic folk had learned
to domesticate animals and to cultivate grain crops; they
were the first farmers and agriculturists, and as a result of
their improved economy were able to live in fairly settled
communities. Having some control over their environment,
they had more opportunity for invention. They made
pottery, some of which was decorated ; they also made
flint sickles for cutting grain, and shaped large stones, known
as querns, for grinding the grain into meal.

Their flint implements also show improvements of form
and technique, the arrow-heads being especially beautiful.
The earlier types are called leaf-shaped, being similar in
shape to birch, willow, and other leaves. Some fine specimens
have been found in and immediately around Watchet, Fig. 3.
The Neolithic axes too were of a greatly improved type,
especially the polished forms of the later period. Unfortunately no complete specimens have been found as yet
in our locality, though portions which have been broken
and re-utilized have come to light. Fig. 3, No. 8 illustrates a
good example of an unpolished axe of the earlier Neolithic
period found at Doniford some few years ago.

The Neolithic people were soon followed by Bronze Age
tribes and somewhat later by Iron Age settlers, the latter
being the Goidels, Brythons and Belgae, who played such
an important part in the Celtic settlement of the West
Country, Wales, Ireland, and Scotland. There are numerous
traces of these people around us, of which the barrow at
Battlegore, Williton, is a good example. Excavated by
Mr. St. George Gray, F.S.A., in 1931, it was found to be an
early Bronze Age barrow. In the fields around the barrow
several bronze implements were dug up during the last
century ; Fig. 4 illustrates three of them.

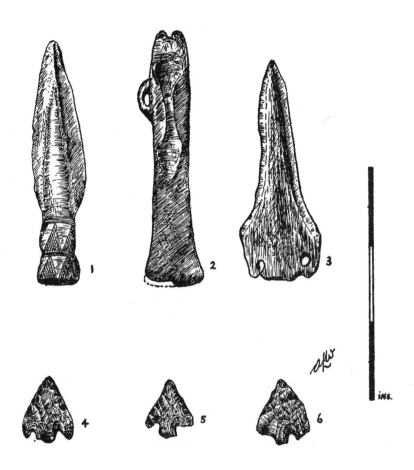

Fig. 4. BRONZE AGE IMPLEMENTS

1. Bronze spear-head (found near Battlegore, Williton).
2. Bronze axe (found near Battlegore, Williton).
3. Bronze dagger (found near Battlegore, Williton).
4. Barbed and tanged arrow-head (Cleeve Hill).
5. Barbed and tanged arrow-head (Nine Elms Nursery, Watchet).
6. Barbed and tanged arrow-head (Williton Hill).

The foregoing evidence of primitive man in this locality makes it appear certain that the site on which Watchet now stands has been known and trodden by man throughout a long period of prehistory, from the time of the Old Stone Age hunters, who were contemporary with the mammoth, to the Iron Age, when the lake-villages at Glastonbury and Meare were probably the cultural centres of civilization in the West Country. Although as yet we can furnish no actual proof, it does not need a great effort of imagination to visualize the little natural harbour of Watchet being used as a trading centre as far back as Bronze and Iron Age times.

From the Roman to the English Conquest

At the time of the Roman Conquest there is little doubt that West Somerset was part of the country held by the Brythonic tribes. Burroughs in his book *Camps of Somerset* suggests that the name of the tribesmen who inhabited Somerset was derived from the lowlands between the Quantocks and the Mendips. This name, *Seo-Mere-Saetan*, which he interprets as ' the dwellers by the sea lakes ', gave them the tribal name of *Sumorsaetas*. The Celtic tribesmen probably lived in small family groups in the neighbourhood where natural conditions were suitable for their farming methods ; they were also likely to have been in contact with the Brythons of South Wales—the British. In fact, there is ample evidence, as far back as the Iron Age people at Glastonbury, that they made sizeable dug-out canoes. Taunton Museum possesses a very fine example, and it seems reasonable to suggest that the Celtic tribes could have established and maintained close contact with South Wales by this means.

Evidence of place and river names also shows that the British left definite traces in West Somerset : a few examples are *Dun*—a hill fort, *Avon* from *Afon*—water, *Tre*—a place or dwelling, *Tun* or *Ton*—an enclosure, while Combe seems certain to be a Saxon form of the old Celtic *Cwm*—a valley.

The derivation of the place-name Watchet has several interpretations ; one suggestion is that the name is derived from the British word *Waesc*, ground washed over by water. While this explanation is interesting it would be wise to treat it with caution. Ekwall in the *Concise Oxford Dictionary of English Place-Names* lists the following variations with sources and dates : *Waeced*, A.D. 918, and *Wecedport*, A.D. 987, both from the *Anglo-Saxon Chronicle* ; *Waecet*, A.D. 962, *Cartularium Saxonicum* ; *Wacet*, *Domesday Book* ; *Wechet*, Asser, A.D. 1243. The earliest form is believed to be identical with the Gaulish *vo-ceto*, which means lower wood. The Gaulish *vo-* corresponds to the Welsh *gwo-* ' under ', while *ceto-* is similar to the Welsh *coed-* ' wood '. Thus we have the town below, or under, the wood. The correctness of this interpretation seems highly probable especially if we remember that all the high ground around Watchet in those days would certainly have been heavily wooded.

It seems doubtful if the early years of the Roman Occupation saw any great changes in the district. The country around, bounded on the east by the Quantocks, to the south by the Brendons and by Exmoor to the west, might easily have been a natural stronghold for the Britons inhabiting the district. Sir Charles Oman, in his *England Before the Conquest*, wrote : ' The notable thing about the map of military Britain furnished by Notitia [a Roman document dated round about A.D. 400] is that no provision whatever seems to have been made for Wales or the south-western regions around the Severn Mouth.' He thought it likely that the Roman government might have handed over the defence of Wales and the West Country to its own inhabitants. This reference is to the closing years of the

Occupation and, whatever the position may have been during the preceding period, it is significant to note that while the areas of the Mendips and south-eastern Somerset are extremely rich in Roman remains (with evidence of roads, villas, coin hoards, etc.), from the mouth of the River Parrett to Exmoor there is as yet little evidence of any important occupation.

We must not assume from this that the Romans had no contact with West Somerset ; Roman coins have been found at Stogursey, Holford, Stogumber, Luxborough, Washford, Dunster Park, North Hill, Minehead, on the Brendon Hills, and even on Dunkery, while a few years ago the writer found a substantial part of a Roman brooch on Cleeve Hill. The most important evidence we have of any settled native occupation during the period is supplied by traces of a Romano-British settlement discovered at Doniford in the winter of 1947. Among material found here were numerous pieces of pottery typical of the period, including some pieces of decorated ware, sherds of cooking-pots and portions of storage-jars. Broken tiles were also discovered, including an almost complete ridging tile and some of the iron nails used for fixing. Among the debris found at the bottom of a small trench, or rubbish pit, were many bones and teeth of animals including those of horse, ox, sheep, pig and red deer. Limpet and winkle shells were plentiful and in one place formed an almost solid mass several inches thick. Only one coin was found : this was a small bronze piece of Constantine A.D. 330–337 which approximately dates the settlement as fourth century.

From the archaeological evidence at our disposal it looks as if the native population might have lived during this time very much as they did previously. No doubt they were influenced to some degree by contact with Roman centres, a suggestion which is borne out by the discovery of a rather fine piece of Samian pottery at Doniford in 1937. This particular type of pottery was manufactured in Gaul and imported into Britain by the Romans, whereas the domestic pottery, such as cooking- and storage-pots, was made in Britain.   In all probability the local Britons, who lived some distance from the main Roman towns and high-ways, continued in the old Celtic traditions as their fore-fathers had done before the Roman Conquest.   The basis of the Celtic tribal life was the kinship or enlarged family group and their whole economic structure centred on the *gwely*, which represented the amount of land that could be worked with one plough and an ox team.   The land was the joint property of the tribe, shared or subdivided among the adult males, each of whom helped in the communal ploughing and harvest.   That they had reached a fairly advanced stage of civilization is shown by their extensive use of iron for tools and agricultural implements, as well as by their useful and in many ways quite artistic pottery.

The Romans began to withdraw their legions from Britain about the end of the fourth century and by the year A.D. 407 the withdrawal was almost complete.   It seems doubtful if this event had much effect on the Britons of our locality, and in all probability their well-established tribal economy and customs continued and life went on very much as before.   Another event that was ultimately to become of the greatest importance to the Britons of the west was the Saxon invasions of A.D. 449.   These invading tribes were composed of Angles, Saxons, and Jutes, the two former being fairly primitive Germanic peoples who came from southern Denmark and from the area round the mouth of the River Elbe.   The Jutes were probably of Frankish origin from the lower Rhineland.

Landing at various points and at different times, the invaders quickly overwhelmed the Britons in the eastern and south-eastern districts of Britain, where they settled for a while. They established their homesteads on the most fertile land, using the native people as slaves. It was not until the year A.D. 577 that they made any serious attempt to conquer the West Country when they fought a pitched battle with the Britons at Deorham near Bath. They defeated the Britons and advanced to the shore of the Severn, thereby cutting off the Britons of the south-west from those of Wales. J. R. Green's map, *Britain in the Midst of the English Conquest*, gives a very clear picture of how the Britons of North Wales (i.e. the whole of Wales as we know it to-day) were cut off from the Britons of West Wales, this being the territory of the *Sumorsaetas* and the *Defnsaetas* who held Somerset, Devon and Cornwall.

For the next two hundred years conditions must have been very unsettled and difficult for the Britons of West Wales. Continual attacks were made by the Saxon kings against them ; first came the campaigns of Cenwealh and then those of Penda. The latter managed in the year A.D. 658 to drive the Britons back to the River Parrett. In the year A.D. 682 the Saxon king Centwine again attacked the Sumorsaetae, pressing them back to the coast west of the river, the victory making the Saxons masters of the Quantocks and probably winning for them the ports of Bridgwater and Watchet. A few years later one of the most successful of the Saxon kings, Ine (A.D. 688–726), conquered a large part of Somerset. He built a fortress on the River Tone to guard the frontiers of his new conquest and this West-Saxon fortress eventually became Taunton. The last strongholds of the British in the west were undoubtedly Exmoor, Devon and Cornwall, and it was not until the year A.D. 815 that the West-Saxon king, Ecgberht, marched into the heart of this region. Even then it took eight years of bitter fighting to conquer the remaining Britons.

By the time Alfred the Great (A.D. 871–901) was ruler
of Wessex it seems probable that Watchet had become an
important Saxon port. The late Rev. W. H. P. Greswell,
who was an authority on the history of the Quantocks,
suggests that Alferode, the old highway which ran over the
Quantocks from Buncombe and Bagborough to Watchet,
was originally Alfred's Road. Further evidence of the
importance of the district is that Cannington, Williton and
Carhampton were all ' Royal Hundreds ' in Saxon times,
the main geographical feature of the Cannington and Williton
Hundreds being the wild forest ground of the Quantocks.

Evidence of the importance of Watchet to the Saxons
is suggested by the fact that it was the site of a Royal Mint.
During Saxon times money in general use was not struck
at a central mint as it is to-day, but was produced by
moneyers in the more important towns. In Somerset coins
were minted at what were then, apparently, the principal
towns, namely Axbridge, Bath, Bruton, Cadbury, Crew-
kerne, Ilchester, Langport, Milborne Port, Petherton,
Taunton, and Watchet. The first of the Saxon kings to
issue coinage from Watchet was Æthelred II, and it is interesting to note that the amount minted during the reign of
this king greatly exceeds in numbers that of any of the
succeeding kings. Coins struck at Watchet which the writer
has been able to trace in museum collections are as follows:
Æthelred 21, Canute 12, Harold 3, Harthacnut 2, Edward
the Confessor 5.

The moneyer was an important official in Saxon times
and the post was usually held by a burgess of the town who
was a man of property and a responsible citizen. The
inscription of his name on the coin guaranteed its genuine-
ness, enabling the King's representatives to check any
irregularities. There appear to have been three moneyers

KEY TO PLATE

No.	King.	Reverse Legend.	Moneyer.
1	ÆTHELRED II	SILERIC M-O PELED.	SIGERIC
2	,,	SILERIC M-O PELED.	,,
3	,,	HVNEPINE M-. PELED	HUNEWINE
4	,,	,,　　　,,　　　,,	,,
5	CNUT (CANUTE)	LODCILD ON PELED.	GODCILD
6	HAROLD I	LODCILD ON PEL.	,,
7	EDWARD CONFESSOR	L.C ON CEPOR.I	LOC
8	EDWARD CONFESSOR	LODCILD ON PECE:	GODCILD
9	WILLIAM I	SIPOLF ON PICDE.	SIWOLF
10	,,	SILOLF ON PICEDI.	SIGOLF
11	WILLIAM II	SIGOVLF ON PICI.	SIGOULF
12	STEPHEN	FO... .ON. WACET.	FO ... ?

PLATE I

COINS OF THE WATCHET MINT

PLATE II

WATCHET HARBOUR IN THE 1860's

at Watchet from the time of Æthelred II to that of Edward the Confessor, their names being Sigeric, Hunewine and Godcild. The currency of the country during the whole of the period of the Watchet mint was the silver penny and no denomination of larger size or value appears to have been issued. Pennies could be cut in half to make half-pennies and quarters (farthings), though as far as we are aware none of these cut pieces is known to have come from Watchet. Plate 1, facing page 20, was kindly prepared by the Department of Coins and Medals of the British Museum for the writer's paper on the Watchet Mint and it will be seen from the key appended that there are several variations in the spelling of Watchet ; the earliest form being PECED. The Saxon character *Win* which looks like a triangular P was used for W until the reign of Stephen when the legend became WACET.

The money minted at Watchet is well dispersed, a high proportion being in museums at Stockholm and Copenhagen. The keeper of the Royal Cabinet Collection at Stockholm, Mr. N. L. Rasmussen, informed the writer that most of the Anglo-Saxon coins came from hoards buried in the later times of the Vikings ; Mr. Georg Galster, of the Danish National Museum, Copenhagen, wrote that several of the Watchet coins in that collection were discovered in hoards at Jutland and Zealand. The reason for this concentration of Anglo-Saxon money in Scandinavia is undoubtedly the levying of the Danegeld by Danish raiders in the tenth and eleventh centuries. It has been estimated that between A.D. 991 and A.D. 1014 the Viking armies received 158,000 pounds of silver, equal to a sum of between £8 to £10 million in modern money. There is every reason to believe that in this considerable amount of tribute collected by the Danes coins minted at Watchet found their way into Scandinavian hoards, and the evidence that we have of raids on Watchet during these unsettled times appears to substantiate this.

The first recorded raid here was that of A.D. 918, mentioned in the *Anglo-Saxon Chronicle* : ' Then nevertheless they [the Danes] stole away by night on some two occasions, once up to the east of Watchet, and on another occasion to Porlock. Then they were beaten on both occasions, so that few of them came away save only those who there swam out to the ships. And these seated themselves out on the island of Flatholm.' A more serious raid is mentioned by Florence of Worcester as having taken place in A.D. 977. He records that the Danes : ' Entered the mouth of the River Severn, and ravaged sometimes Cornwall, sometimes North Wales, and then Watchet in Devonshire, and there brought great evil in burning and man-slaying.'

A most interesting account of a raid on the Watchet district is given in a tract, believed to have been written by Robert Gay (1631–72), parson of Nettlecombe. Here is an extract from the document : ' The 4th Invasion (A.D. 988) was apud Wecheport, alias Wechport, (i.e.) Watchett. Thus the heathonish Danes having left Britaine, for the space of 19 years, at length returned hither, under the command of Otherus and Rhoaldus their generalls, and having sailed round Cornwall, came into Seaverne, plundered and burnt upon the Sea-Coast wheresoever they had opportunity, but the king had disposed his Armie into convenient places of defence from the River Avon, which runs through Bristoll, along the Sea Coasts to Cornwall, notwithstanding the Danes brake into Watchett by stealth in the night, plundered and burnt the same, and then they marched toward the other part thereof [which must be Williton], where a part of the Kings Armie using [issuing] out of their fortifications, there met them, as they were coming encountered them, and

slew a great number on the place, pursued the rest to
Watchett, and slew as many as could not swime to the
shipps.   But the Anglo-Saxons Duke, or generall, Godman
and their valiant Champion Streame Guld, and divers others
of the Kings Armie were slain also.'   Then follows an account
of Battlegore, referred to as Grabburrowes, and the probability, according to the author, of this site being the burial
place of the Anglo-Saxon slain.   As this legend still persists
locally it is as well to quote the following remarks from the
conclusion of Mr. St. George Gray's report of the Battlegore
excavations, ' The former notion that the place marked the
site of a conflict with the Danes in A.D. 918 (or at any other
date) has certainly not been proved, in fact no remains of
the period have been found in that portion of Battlegore
which has been examined, and of the previous " finds " made
there or in the adjoining fields, namely, six implements of
bronze, all have reference to the Bronze Age, dating from
the earliest part of the period down to the time of the
" socketed celt " [Cast bronze axe].'

The last recorded raid on Watchet appears to have
taken place in the year A.D. 997 ; this is mentioned in the
Anglo-Saxon Chronicle and the account ends thus : ' . . .
great evil in burning and man-slaying being wrought.   The
Danes eventually withdrew.'

In his *Early Wars of Wessex* Albany Major put forward
some interesting theories regarding Watchet during the
period of the English Conquest.   One was that Watchet was
a trading settlement of the Norsemen, situated at the mouth
of the valley.   He was of the opinion that it might have
been the only route from the Severn Sea into Dyvaint (the
British territory which included Devon, and part of Dorset
and Somerset west of the River Parrett), and he suggested
that Williton (the town of the Welshmen) lying on this road
derived its name from the occupants of Watchet.   He wrote :

' The sharp racial definition implied by the name renders it almost certain that here at Williton was the guarded point at which the British traders from Dyvaint met the outland seafaring merchants from the haven which they occupied.' He also suggested that during the eighth and ninth centuries the Danes were allies of the Britons against the Anglo-Saxons and that they helped them to resist the growing pressure of these invaders. In support of this he wrote, ' It was only after the whole western peninsula had become Saxon that the Danes marauded in the lands of their old allies. The presumption that the friendship, and friendly settlement of the coasts, was of ancient standing, and that here also was a mixed race as in Ireland is very strong.'

With the evidence of the Saxon mint and the raids alone, we can say with some degree of certainty that Watchet was a place of importance during the later period of the English Conquest. By this time the old tribal structure had virtually been broken up and the system of Shires, Hundreds and Townships was well established. Generally the country seems to have been moving towards feudalism, and the movement was probably quickened when the custom was introduced, in the tenth century, of placing groups of shires under the control of earls. These men, ruling large territories, appear to have been very powerful ; they were in fact petty kings, sometimes coming into conflict with the central government and the king.

Unfortunately for the archaeologist the Saxons seem to have been poor builders, in contrast to the Romans who came before them and with the Normans who followed them, and their dwellings have nowhere survived. We know, from the evidence of the few villages and dwelling-sites that have been excavated in Britain, that their dwellings were rather miserable and squalid huts with walls constructed of mud and straw. In the middle of the floor of a typical hut was a clay hearth with stones, and around this were post-holes which held the roof supports. The important buildings must have been rather more substantially built with stouter timber for roofs and doors, and if we allow our imaginations to carry us back to the Watchet of this period, we may catch a glimpse of the moneyers Sigeric or Hunewine busy making silver pennies for Æthelred or Canute in just such a building.

Around the small harbour we can imagine men repairing and building ships ; traders unloading their ships and loading goods on to pack animals for the journey over the Quantock trackways to the towns and villages of the interior. The countryside generally would have been much more densely wooded than it is to-day and only around the towns and villages should we have seen cleared ground. The farms and arable land would be very close to, or even inside, the town boundary. On the land about the town we should probably have seen some of the conquered Britons working as slaves for their Saxon masters, and on the wilder and more remote districts of Exmoor we might still have seen small groups, remnants of the British tribes, ekeing out an existence by hunting and primitive agriculture. Evidence of Celtic influences from Exmoor to Land's End is still fairly plentiful and the Celtic language is known to have been spoken in Cornwall as late as the eighteenth century.

ST. DECUMAN'S CHURCH, WATCHET, c. 1875

CHAPTER TWO

MEDIEVAL WATCHET

The Norman Conquest and the Middle Ages

THE LANDING of William of Normandy in A.D. 1066, and the fighting which followed, was too remote from Watchet to have had any immediate effect, though there is on record an incident connected with the defeat of the English. This is said to have occurred at Watchet in A.D. 1067 when Gytha, the widow of Earl Godwin and the mother of King Harold (who was killed at Senlac, Hastings, during the battle between his army and that of the Normans), embarked at Watchet with her ladies for the Steep Holm. There, according to report, they stayed some time mourning the fallen fortunes of her family, before sailing to St. Omer in Brittany.

The military victories of William I were later to have important repercussions on local government and economy of the town and villages around. In the Shire organizations of the Saxons we could see the early forms of feudalism developing, and now we see the actual imposition of feudal government on the whole countryside. Within a few years the whole of the English landowners had been dispossessed of their lands by William, who now became the sole owner. He, in turn, made grants of land to his followers in return for military services or payment of dues. With these grants of land went the political right to govern the cultivators, also the right to levy taxes, to exact services, and to hold courts of justice. The King's chief concern was that his vassals should be in a position to supply him with soldiers in time of war.

Twenty years after the Conquest William I ordered a survey to be taken of the whole country and sent commissioners to visit practically every town, village and hamlet. The commissioners called together the leading men of the town or village to examine them and obtain all the information required about their locality. They questioned the villagers as to the extent of the land, its value, the holders, and the numbers of horses, cattle, sheep and pigs. The objects of this survey, named the Domesday, were twofold ; the first was to obtain the information necessary for levying the geld, or property tax ; the second to give the King detailed knowledge of the wealth, lands, and income of his vassals.

Watchet is mentioned in the Exon (Exeter) Domesday survey as being part of the land of William de Moion. This is the de Moion, or de Mohun, who built the original fortress at Dunster. It is recorded that William the Conqueror granted de Moion the Manor of *Torre* (Dunster) with sixty-seven others, and Watchet, or land at Watchet, was one of those grants. According to the Rev. R. W. Eyton's *Domesday Studies of Somerset*, de Moion had given Dudeman sub-tenure of his land at *Wacet* (Watchet) as well as at Stogumber, Elworthy and other places. The Domesday reference to Watchet is as follows :

'The same Dudeman holds of William the Sheriff *Wacet*. Alwold held it T.R.E. and paid geld for one virgate of land. There is land for half a plough. Nevertheless there is 1 plough with 1 serf and 1 bordar and 1 riding horse. There is a mill paying 10 shillings. It is worth 15 shillings. When William received it, 5 shillings.'

What this means is that Dudeman holds, or rents, *Wacet* from the Sheriff, William de Moion. Alwold, the former Saxon owner held it T.R.E., i.e., *tempore Regis Edwardi*. The date of the Domesday survey is A.D. 1086 and the King Edward (the Confessor), to whose time it refers as T.R.E., died 5th January, 1066. The 'hide' was the unit of assessment on which the geld was paid, its sub-divisions were the 'virgate', one quarter of the hide, the 'ferling' (farthing), one quarter of the virgate.

It is obvious from the Domesday survey that Watchet was quite unimportant agriculturally, ' 1 plough with 1 serf and 1 bordar' makes it appear a very small estate, especially when compared with others in the district. For example the Domesday record of Withycombe reads : ' Edmer holds of the bishop [of Coutances] *Widicumbe.* Alnod held it T.R.E. when it was assessed to the geld for three hides. The arable land is sufficient for ten ploughs. There are in the demesne two ploughs and six bordmen Fourteen villeins and seven bordars have eight ploughs. There are ten acres of meadow, five hundred and fifty acres of pasture, and ninety-six acres of wood.'

The contrast is seen even more sharply with the record of the Royal Hundreds of Cannington, Williton, and Car-hampton, which are described conjointly in Domesday ; these had land sufficient for one hundred ploughs. An extract from the record reads : ' There are eleven ploughs and a half in the demesne, and eleven bondmen, and thirty coliberti and thirty-eight villeins, and fifty bordars, who have thirty-seven ploughs and a half.'

The evidence that Watchet was such a small agricultural unit, compared with Withycombe, Williton and others in the district, suggests that the inhabitants of the town were chiefly concerned with trade and commerce. This explan-ation seems to be quite possible in view of the fact that the Royal Mint founded by the Saxon Kings was still in operation, minting money for William I (the Conqueror), William II, and Stephen, in turn.

It might be desirable at this point to give a general picture of the structure of feudalism. At the time of the Domesday survey slaves had become a rapidly vanishing class; they were usually the servants or ploughmen of the lords, but the lords were finding it more economical to hire personal attendants and to work the demesne lands with the forced labour of the serfs. The bordars and cottars were the holders of small patches of land outside the open-field system; most of them were serfs, but a number were reckoned as free tenants.

The villeins usually held approximately fifteen-acre or thirty-acre shares in the common fields and were perhaps the most important subjects of the lord of the manor. Their services were of two kinds, day-work and boon-work. ' Day-work ' meant that a number of days in each week must be devoted to work on the lord's land (the demesne); usually this work lasted for three days. ' Boon-work ' consisted of extra labour which could be demanded by the lord at any time; obviously it was very unpopular as the demand usually came at sheep-shearing or harvest time when a serf's labour was badly needed on his own land.

In addition to these heavy demands on their labour-services the villeins were also subject to certain bans and monopolies: they were not allowed to grind their own corn, which had to go to the lord's mill where the villeins were compelled to pay a certain proportion of their grain for the miller's service; baking, too, often had to be done in the village bakery. The lord of the manor claimed exclusive rights over the village waste-land, and where these rights were enforced rigidly it meant that the villein could cut no wood or turf and would have no pasture for his swine. Any land reclaimed from the waste was added to the lord's demesne.

Pope Innocent III, a contemporary of King John, aptly summed up the life of a serf at this period when he wrote : ' The serf serves, he is terrified with threats, wearied by *corvees* [forced services], afflicted with blows, despoiled of his possessions, for if he possesses nought he is compelled to earn, and if he possesses anything he is compelled to have it not, the lord's fault is the serf's punishment, the serf's fault is the lord's excuse for preying on him . . . '

While the lords and their clerks did their utmost to apply these laws generally, in practice there was much modification by custom and on the average manor the serf had a certain ' rough ' security.

The struggle between the Norman lawyers and the serfs went on for two centuries at least ; in the early days the lawyers made substantial gains, but they were never able to advance beyond a certain point because there were customary rights that the serf would not relinquish ; during the thirteenth century economic forces began to help the peasants and eventually transformed them into free wage-labourers, or small-holders, paying rents for their land instead of giving services as they had been doing for generations. This continual conflict between the lords and the peasants must be borne in mind if we are to interpret the political history of the period.

The Borough and Medieval Landowners

From the scanty and scattered information obtainable relating to the feudal and medieval periods at Watchet it is difficult to present as complete a picture as one could wish of the little community there and how it fared during the three or four centuries that followed the Norman Conquest. Watchet's history during that time does not fall into such a well-defined pattern as, for example, that of Dunster with its Norman lords, the de Mohuns, dominating and directing its fortunes from their castle stronghold for over three centuries and then giving place to the Luttrells whose régime has lasted from 1404 to the present day. What we find in the case of Watchet is a succession of families, some of them bearing names of no little note in their day, with possessive interests more or less extensive but none of them apparently residing in Watchet or exercising any sort of perceivable influence likely to promote beneficial results.

It is true that quite early in this stage of Watchet's story we often find it called a borough. ' The Burgh of Wechet comes by twelve', wrote the recording scribe when King Henry the Third's itinerant justices held an eyre, or court, at Ilchester in 1242. That is to say the borough sent twelve burgesses or representatives to this eyre at which Albreda [Aubrey] de Wechet appealed that William Cute, Robert Russepin, John la Wayte, William the Baker, and Andrew of the churchyard were guilty of a breach ' of the peace of our lord the King and of robbery'. (' Somersetshire Pleas '—Somerset Record Society, Vol. II.) In a deed dated the forty-third year of Edward III (1368-9) there is mention of ' the Commonalty of the Borough of Watchet', which suggests that the town had at that time some form of local government. Such circumstances would imply the grant of a charter at an early date but no record of any such privilege has yet been found. It is possible that Watchet may have been what is sometimes termed ' a borough by prescription,' i.e., a borough which was never established by charter but which, for various reasons, came to be recognized as entitled to such status. It is also on record that in the year 1302 the ' Burrough of Wechet ' was summoned to send two representatives to Parliament, they were William Clarke, Jnr., and Walter de Portbury.

It must have been a very hazardous undertaking to journey from Watchet to London in those days. The roads

had for centuries been a constant source of worry to the
central government and to the landowners. In the year
1285 Edward I ordered that highways to market-towns
should be enlarged and cleared of underwood for a space
of two hundred feet on each side to prevent ambuscades of
highway robbers. In the next century the roads again
fell into decay, probably owing to the shortage of labour
resulting from the decimation of the population by the
great plagues, and to the lack of money occasioned by heavy
expenditure on Edward the Third's wars. In fact the
state of the roads became so bad in the years 1331, 1339,
and 1380, that Parliaments were adjourned because it was
impossible for members to attend.

There is frequent mention in the records of this period
to Watchet, or the parish of St. Decuman's, being ' ancient
demesne of the Crown'. This is explained by the fact that
the whole parish, except for one virgate in Watchet and
three hides elsewhere, was in the Royal manor of Williton,
which was one of the twelve manors in Somerset held by
King Edward the Confessor at his death. The ' one virgate '
excepted might possibly be identified with that portion
which Dudeman, after the Conquest, held of William de
Mohun. Early in the twelfth century the rest of the parish
became the property of William de Falaise, a Norman on
whom William the Conqueror bestowed Stoke (Courcy) and
Wootton (Courtenay), and other manors in Dorset and
Wiltshire. De Falaise, enriched by marriage to a wealthy
widow, was able to purchase, somewhere between 1100 and
1107, the Royal manor of Williton. On his death the manor
passed to his younger daughter, Sybil, who married a Suffolk
knight, Baldwin de Boulers. One of their two daughters,
Maud, became the wife of Richard Fitzurse of Williton,
about 1140, bringing to him part of the Falaise estates in
Somerset, including the Royal manor of Williton. Richard

Fitzurse was the father of Reginald or Reynold de Fitzurse, who was one of the murderers of Thomas à Beckett.

By a special charter, which is still preserved at Dunster Castle, Reginald de Fitzurse granted to his brother Robert a moiety [a half share] of the manor, the other moiety having been granted to the Knights Templars in alms for his soul. When the male line of the Fitzurse family came to an end with the death of Sir Ralph Fitzurse, the grandson of Robert, in 1350, it was found that he was possessed, with Maud, his wife, of among other estates the manor of Williton and the borough of Watchet. There was still in existence then a younger branch of the Fitzurse family, who also had interests in Watchet and Doniford, the last of these, John Fitzurse, in 1369, effected a settlement of land at Wolrichislonde on himself and Joan his wife and their heirs. In default of issue this land was to go to the ' Commonalty of the Borough of Watchet ' in aid of the maintenance of a chaplain to celebrate in the Chapel of the Holy Cross, there to pray for the good of the souls of John Fitzurse's parents, himself and his wife, and their children.

Dame Maud Fitzurse, the widow of Sir Ralph, died in 1389 possessed of, among other rights, ' a yearly rent from the tenants of the manor of Watchet', the Fitzurse holdings were then divided between the co-heirs of Sir Ralph, these were James Durburgh (whose father had, in 1344, married Sir Ralph's daughter Hawis) and Sir Ralph's great-grandchildren, Willema and Joan. James Durburgh received a quarter of the manor of Williton and Watchet. The family, which took its name from a place in Stoke Courcy parish, had previously acquired land and property in Watchet by marriage and purchase, and a deed of 1375 (Dunster Castle muniments) records a grant by Sir John de Ralegh, of Nettlecombe, to Sir Hugh de

Durburgh and Hawis, his wife, of a tenement in Watchet
' on the west side of the street called Swynstret'.

Early in the fifteenth century the male line of the
Durburgh's became extinct. The younger daughter of the
last of them, by marriage with Alexander Hadley of Withycombe, about 1430, brought part of the Durburgh possessions
in Watchet to that family. One of Alexander's descendants,
James, in 1527, conveyed the manor of Williton, and property
in Watchet, to feofees [public trustees] for the administration of his will which was remarkable for the great
number of legacies to monasteries, churches (including St.
Decuman's), priests, and other ecclesiastics in West Somerset.
The last male of the family, Arthur, who died in 1538,
married Eleanor, daughter of Sir John Wyndham, of Orchard
Wyndham.

Other records show to what extent various properties
in Watchet were acquired by different families during the
twelfth, thirteenth, and fourteenth centuries. For example,
during the reign of Henry II (1154–1189) Richard Fitzurse
granted the manor of Doniford, with appurtenances in
Watchet, to William de Regni, of Aisholt, on service of a
knight's fee. While in the early part of the next century
Ralph Fitzwilliam, of Withycombe, a descendant of one of
the de Mohuns, had interests there—incidentally, he was
fined twenty marks in 1210 because his wife Yolenta and
his reeve Walter, had caused some merchants of Flanders
to be arrested at Watchet. The Fitzwilliam property passed
to Ralph's grand-daughter, Isabel, who in 1236 married
Hugh Peverel. In 1280 their son John quit-claimed to
Robert Martin and his wife Amy (grand-daughter of Isabel
Peveral) all rights in his land at Watchet. Robert Martin's
younger son and his wife, Isabel, sold in 1329 the reversion
of the estate to Ralph Fitzurse. The Martin family owned
several manors elsewhere ; their memory is preserved in

the names of Combe Martin in Devon, and Compton Martin in Somerset. A branch of the Luttrells of East Quantoxhead also acquired land in Watchet early in the fourteenth century.

From the Assize Rolls we learn that in the year 1354 Alexander Luttrell, grandson of the first Luttrell of East Quantoxhead who was knighted by Edward III at his coronation in 1327, was killed at Watchet, together with Alexander Montfort and John Strechleye. Several persons were found guilty of murder, and others were declared to have been present and assisting. A very interesting story probably lies behind this incident, but we lack, however, any details that would give us a reason as to why some inhabitants of Watchet should have murdered Alexander Luttrell and his companions.

Around the middle of the fourteenth century there is evidence that the de Brito or de Bret family from whom Sampford Brett took its second name, had a rent of £4 from property in Watchet. One of them, Edmund, and his wife Alice, conveyed this in 1359 to Hugh Courtenay, Earl of Devon, and Margaret his wife and their sons. The rent probably derived from a small manor carved out of Watchet, the manor of Culvercliffe, was received by the Courtenays for more than four centuries, and in support of this claim we have it recorded that Philip Courtenay, who died in 1611, held the manor of Culvercliffe from George Luttrell, of Dunster Castle, ' by fealty and service unknown'.

Two other West Somerset families also acquired various land in Watchet during the fifteenth and sixteenth centuries. The Jewe's of Wiveliscombe in 1410, and the Sydenham's of Orchard (Williton) in the reign of Henry VII. In a will dated 1557 Sir John Sydenham left to his younger son John various lands which included the borough of Watchet. Sir John had also acquired by purchase, Kentsford, which he left to his wife. The male line of Sydenhams at Orchard became extinct with the younger son John, and with the marriage of his younger daughter and co-heiress, Elizabeth, to Sir John Wyndham, the estate of Orchard became designated as Orchard Wyndham. From that time all the pieces of property comprising Watchet and the parish of St. Decuman's were eventually brought together to form again, after several centuries, a complete manorial entity, a circumstance which has probably been conducive to the later development and progress of the town.

Agriculture

We have seen how in Saxon and Norman times the towns and villages were surrounded by arable land, pastures, and woods ; and the farms were not isolated as we usually find them to-day, but were actually in, and part of, the town. The early form of tillage was that of the open-field system, whereby strips of land were cultivated, separated not by hedges or fences but by a narrow unploughed strip called a ' baulk ' ; until recent years there were a number of these strips with baulks at Wristland.

The medieval acre was a narrow strip of land, forty rods in length and four rods in width ; the half-acre was the same length, but only two rods in width. The most common method of cultivation was the three-field system, which meant that for the first year a number of strips were sown to wheat, rye, or some other crop in the autumn and harvested in the following summer. Other strips would be planted with oats, barley, or peas in the spring and harvested in the same year. The remaining strips would be allowed to lie fallow during the season in order for them to regain their fertility. The following year this fallow land would be sown with wheat, etc. ; the wheat strips of the previous year would be devoted to oats or barley ; and the previous oat and barley strips would be allowed to lie fallow—so the cropping rotation would go on.

Agriculture in earlier times was extremely crude ; wheat and rye were grown for the making of bread ; barley grown chiefly for brewing beer, which we must remember was the common beverage ; peas and beans, although sometimes used for food, were usually grown for use as cattle-food. Potatoes were, of course, unknown, while root crops and fresh vegetables were little cultivated. Meadow land was regarded as extremely valuable, being estimated at several times the value of arable land. No clover or grass mixtures for dry ground were known and the hay crop from the meadows was the main food supply for the oxen, horses, and breeding animals during the winter months. Under these conditions it was impossible to keep many stock animals during the winter months and the only alternative course was to kill the surplus animals during the autumn and to salt down the meat. This practice was generally resorted to and it is believed to have been responsible for the great number of scurvy and skin diseases which were common among all classes in the Middle Ages.

Summer grazing was done on the fallow land and, after the harvest, on the stubble, though the largest amount was on the common pasture, where herdsmen or shepherds looked after the animals. At Watchet these common pastures were almost certainly situated to the west of the town, where there is still one large field known as ' the common '. In all probability, before the Enclosure Acts, the whole of the Cleeve Hill area was common land, where the small-holders and farmers grazed their cows, pigs, sheep, and geese. Most of the ploughing was done by oxen ; I have been told by some of the older Watchet people that they have heard their parents say they could remember oxen being used for ploughing at Snailholt Farm, which would bring the use of oxen

well into the nineteenth century, and Mr. G. F. Luttrell of
Dunster still possesses an ox plough of this date. This
evidence is supported by the fairly common occurrence of
ox cues in the local fields, these being in two pieces which
can be nailed on either side of the cleft hoof ; a local farmer
informed me that he has found quite a number on his land
during the past few years.

There is every reason to believe that the valuable
meadow land of Watchet ran up the valley to Kentsford
Farm. and beyond, as it does now ; and that the oldest
arable, or cultivated, ground was to the east and south of
the town. The tithe map of 1841 shows a number of strip
cultivations still in existence and it is quite possible that
these fields had remained almost unaltered since Saxon
times. The largest group of strips covered most of the
present Memorial Ground and ran to the edge of the cliff
on the Pleasure Grounds, (the railway was cut through these
fields about 1861) ; this group consisted of twenty strips
and was named ' In Culvercliffe '. On the northern side of
Doniford road adjoining these fields were several small
plots named collectively ' Little Wristland', while on the
opposite side of the road was ' Great Wristland', another
large group of strip cultivations.

Strip fields also covered the area from Liddimore Road
to South Road, including the site on which the County
School now stands ; on the opposite side of the road, now
the site of the Church of England School, strips ran all the
way along the ridge to Parsonage Farm.

One great disadvantage of the strip, or open-field,
system of arable cultivation must have been the damage
caused to the crops by straying animals. This menace was
at any rate partially solved in medieval times by the establishment of ' pounds ' in which straying animals were placed,
to be redeemed by their owners on payment of a customary

fine and compensation for damage done. Another reason
for impounding animals is given in the Court Leet records
on page 77. The Watchet Pound, remains of which still
exist, was situated at the corner of South Road and Malvern
Road and was still used for the purpose of shutting up stray
animals until the early years of the present century.

Some of the old field names have been perpetuated in
the terrace names; Gillham Terrace is built at the top of
a field known formerly as ' Gillham's Croft ', that sloped
towards Swain Street, and Almyr Terrace covers a strip of
land named ' In Almerscroft ', which is evidently the piece
referred to as Almascroft in the Court Leet's records of
1747 (see page 77). A careful survey of the old fields of
Watchet should be of great interest as field names can often
give clues to medieval use and ownership; this research,
however, must await a more favourable opportunity. The
following names are selected from the Tithe Apportionment
List of the early nineteenth century: Bondsground, Bell-
ground, Kingsland, Barnsclose, Pulpits Three Acres, Three
Cornered Pulpit, The George Meadow, Five Bells Croft,
Monkey Meadow, Ingram's Meadow, Louseland and Folly
Field.

The Manor

The estate of the lord, known as the Manor, was in
medieval times a small world in itself. Economically and
socially it played a predominant part in the life of the people,
most of whom shared in the labours of the ' demesne ' lands.
The *demesne* land was that directly held by the lord of the
manor: usually it was scattered in plots among the strips
of the open fields and was cultivated by the same methods.
The villeins, cottars, bordars, and serfs were all compelled
to give a substantial amount of their labour to ploughing,
sowing, and harvesting on the demesne land, as well as
hedging, ditching, herding sheep and swine. On an average

more than half of the ordinary peasant's time must have
been given in the service of the lord of the manor; the rest
he could spend on his own plots. The effect of this extremely
arduous life with its economic dependence on the lord of the
manor resulted in the creation of a servile class which,
isolated in small village groups, resisted change for a long
period.

Early in the thirteenth century a process of commutation began : this meant the replacement of labour services
by quit rents, a rent related not to the value of land but to
services. At first day-labour was commuted, then boon-
labour; the lords' frequent need of money sometimes suggested
commutation, at other times the initiative came from the
villagers who felt that money payments were less servile.
The decimation of the population due to the Black Death
accelerated this partial emancipation of the peasantry ; for
the mortality among the labourers was so great that those
left were able to dictate terms to the lords which in most
cases meant a real rise in their living standards. Although
the people of Watchet were probably less dependent on the
manor than those of the surrounding district which was
purely agricultural, the fact that Watchet is referred to in
early records as the ' Town and Burrough ' clearly shows
that trade and industry were of great importance, although
the manor must also have played a considerable part both
socially and economically in the life of the people.

The Manor House of Watchet was Kentsford and
undoubtedly it is the oldest secular building in the parish ;
like most old buildings stories and legends are associated
with the house. It is reputed to have derived its name
from Keyna or Caine, a British virgin who became a Celtic
missionary ; she is described as the daughter of Braghanus,
a Celtic chief, and so was a maiden of noble descent. It
was her custom, so the story goes, to baptize the heathen at

the ford, close by the old pack-horse bridge. This bridge
was built very much later than Keyna's time, of course,
though the builders might have known the story, for let
into the wall of the bridge is a stone cross which may have
been put there to commemorate her memory.

Among early grants of land connected with Kentsford
is one made by Geoffrey Loni, Vicar of St. Decuman's, to
John Basynges, ' of lands at Canisford in the forty-first
year of Edward III ' (1256). In the thirteenth century a
grant of land at ' Kanesford ' was made by Hamo de
Basynges to his son William, and later in the second year
of Henry IV (1400), a grant was made by William Powton
and Richard Orchard to Gilbert Basynges. In this same
year there seems to have been some trouble between the
Basynges family and the Church, for the Patent Rolls, 8th
Nov., 1400, state : ' Westminster Commission to Gournay,
Ivo Fitzwaryn, John Loterell, Baldwin Malet, John Wadham,
William Stourton, and John Manyngford, to enquire into
the report that John, Abbot of Clyve [Cleeve Abbey],
brothers Lythenerstoke, William Pulton and John Harewade,
his fellow monks and Walter Barwick and William Clerk
of Watchet and others to the number of two hundred . . .
went armed on Whitsuntide last to Kentsford, County
Somerset, and there assaulted Gilbert Basynges and cut
down and carried away his trees and underwood.' Unfortunately we do not know the reason for this assault, or
the findings of the commission. The Gilbert Basynges
mentioned died without issue in the year 1437 and his sister
Eleanor ' levied a fine of the same to the trustees for the
use of Richard Luttrell Esquire'.

This Richard Luttrell, who held Kentsford and other
land in Watchet, was Constable of Dunster Castle for some
twenty years from 1430. On his death, without issue, this
estate escheated to his overlord, James Luttrell, of Dunster

Castle. During the reign of Edward VI, Sir John Luttrell sold Kentsford to Sir John Wyndham of Orchard Wyndham, who had acquired Orchard Wyndham by his marriage to Elizabeth, daughter and heiress of Sir John Sydenham. His eldest son John married Florence Wadham, sister of Nicholas Wadham, founder of Wadham College, Oxford.

It was this Florence Wyndham who was the heroine of the well-known Kentsford Legend. The story goes that she was taken ill with a mysterious fit about a year after her marriage, and in the belief that she was dead she was buried in a vault in St. Decuman's Church. During the night the sexton, knowing that some valuable rings were on her fingers, returned to the church, opened the coffin and tried to remove the rings. Finding the rings difficult to remove, he took a knife and started cutting a finger, but to his horror he saw blood appear and the body of the lady move ; this frightened him so much that he immediately fled, leaving his lantern behind. Florence Wyndham, who was now wide awake, picked up the lantern and in her grave clothes walked down the path to Kentsford, where apparently she had great difficulty in persuading her terrified household that she was not a ghost but a reality. Shortly afterwards she gave birth to a son, and it is said that from this son every living member of the family has descended. Although an interesting story, no credence can be placed on it for in many parts of the country, as far apart as Yorkshire, Derbyshire, London, and Cornwall, a similar legend is told of other families with almost identical details.

During the Civil War Sir Edmund Wyndham fought on the side of Charles, and about 1644 he besieged the town and castle of Taunton, held by Colonel Blake for Parliament. Blake was later relieved by a strong Parliamentary force which broke through the besiegers. In 1645 Sir, Edmund was governor of Bridgwater Castle, which was later taken

by storm.   After the restoration of Charles II Sir Edmund
represented Bridgwater in Parliament.   The last of the
family to live at Kentsford appears to have been Charles
Wyndham during the reign of James II.   Eventually the
manor reverted to the senior branch of the family at Orchard
Wyndham.

St. Decuman's Church

The proximity of the Somerset coast to South Wales
and the Celtic origin of a large number of its inhabitants
probably made the coastal areas very fertile ground for the
early Christian missionaries of South Wales.   There seems
to be little doubt that Saint Decombes (Decumanus), who
settled at Watchet, was an active Celtic missionary and an
organizer of Christian monasteries.   Camden wrote : ' Near
the castle of Dunster aforesaid, are two small villages,
dedicated to two of their Country saints : Carenton [Car-
hampton] is the name of the one, from Carentocus the
Britain ; the other, St. Decombes, from Decumanus who,
setting sail out of South Wales, landed here (as we find in
an ancient Agonal) in a horrid desert full of shrubs and
briars, the woods thick and close, stretched out a vast way
both in length and breadth, strutting up with lofty mountains,
severed wonderfully by the hollow vallies.   Here, having
bid farewell to the vanities of the world, he was stabbed by
an Assassin, and so got the reputation of a Saint among
the common people.'

There seem to be few saints without a legend and St.
Decuman is no exception.   The story of his crossing the
Channel on a hurdle, or cloak, with a cow which provided
him with milk in all his wanderings is not uncommon in
saintly legend, and the account of his decapitation and the
subsequent replacement of his head at the holy well can
often be paralleled.

The Church of St. Decuman stands in a commanding position on the highest point of the ridge that runs from the Doniford valley to Kentsford farm. Its tower overlooks the town and sea, and from it almost all the land bounded by the Quantocks, the Brendons, and Exmoor can be seen ; it must certainly have been an excellent vantage point during an emergency. The present building is one of the largest in the neighbourhood. It is mainly Perpendicular in style and has undoubtedly developed from an earlier building dating from the thirteenth century. It has been suggested that a prototype of the church existed as early as A.D. 400, but there appears to be no evidence to support this either archaeologically or from ecclesiastical records. The earliest documentary evidence regarding the church relates to the gift by Simon Brito of the church as a perpetual prebend quit of service, to Wells Cathedral. Dr. Eeles in his book St. Decuman's dates this as being somewhere around the year 1190.

Of the building itself the most important feature is probably the battlemented tower, which is in three stages ; a niche on the south side contains a figure holding a cross, generally considered to represent St. Decuman. The outer walls of the south and north aisles shows the latter with much more decorated battlements to be of more recent construction. A number of carved grotesques are evident, while at the west and north doors are some imperfect water stoups. The pavement of the south porch is quite unusual, having been constructed by setting old roof tiles vertically in the ground. The chancel is the oldest portion of the edifice and parts of it are undoubtedly remains of the thirteenth-century building. The central passage of the chancel floor is covered by thirteenth-century inlaid tiles which are ornamented with shields, arms, and other devices of various Somerset families. Dr. Eeles writes, 'There is

every reason to believe that these tiles were actually made
at Cleeve Abbey and sold to local churches. They are of
the same character as those which form the magnificent
floor of the earlier refectory there.'

The waggon roofs of the church are considered one of
its most interesting features ; the earliest is probably that
of the south aisle, dating from the fifteenth century. This
roof is ornamented with carved bosses, and at the feet of
the braces on the south side are carved angels holding scrolls
ornamented with shields and books, while on the north side
they hold such instruments as a hammer, rope, nails and a
cross.   The north chapel, usually known as the Wyndham
Chapel, contains a number of monuments of this family
and the tombs and effigies of many of the persons mentioned
in the records of Kentsford may be found here. There are
some particularly good examples of monumental brasses,
those of Sir John Windham (1574) and his wife Elizabeth
(1571) being extremely interesting.   The first shows in
excellent detail the armour of a knight of the period, and the
costume of his wife is a beautiful example of a lady's dress
at that time.   The hair, parted in the middle, is covered by
a French hood (a form of head-covering that later developed
into the ' Mary, Queen of Scots' head-dress), the high pleated
collar of the chemisette is surmounted by a small ruff and
the sleeves of the same garment, which are slashed and puffed,
are finished at the wrists with small ruffles. The over-gown
is held at the waist by a cord from which hangs a jewelled
pendant and the front of the skirt is open to show an
embroidered petticoat.   Those of John Windham (1572)'
and Florence (1596), his wife, are also unusually good for
details of costume.

Another monument of high artistic value, as well as
it being of a type that is extremely rare in this country,
is that to the left beneath the east window of the north

chancel. It shows two murals of Sir John Windham (1645) and his wife Joan (1633), and the work is attributed to Nicholas Stone, a master mason to James I and Charles I.

The screens of St. Decuman's are of considerable interest, the section across the south aisle being the oldest ; and it is thought possible that this was originally situated further west connecting with the remains of a staircase in the new aisle wall. The main section of the screen is of later date, and parts, such as the two southern bays of the central section, are modern. The north aisle section was removed by a former Earl of Egremont and a photograph taken before 1886 shows a flat arch forming an opening in the west side of the Egremont pew which occupied the south side of the chancel. Traces of colour can still be seen on the screens : a black-and-white twist on the shafts of some of the uprights as well as red colouring in some of the panels.

The old octagonal font, which has been brought back to replace a modern font made of Devonshire marble presented to the church in 1896, has a plain bowl with narrow moulding above and below supported with carved angels with outstretched wings. The octagonal stem is ornamented with panels, on alternate pairs of which are small shields in relief ; the whole rests on an octagonal base with simple mouldings. Expert opinion considers that originally the font was painted.

The church plate consists of four pieces, one cup of which is of unusual shape; although there are no marks or engraved date, it is considered to be the oldest. The bowl is bell shaped with a spreading lip and is decorated with an Elizabethan leaf ornament. It was formerly thought that the cup was Elizabethan, with a later stem and foot; the whole cup, however, is now believed to date from this period. The second cup is of great size, being twelve inches high

and weighing twenty-nine ounces, avoirdupois. It is inscribed 'Saynt Decuman's 1634'. There are also two patens
of the same date.

Six bells hang in the belfry of St. Decuman's, the oldest
of which is the third. This bell has the mark of Robert
Norton of Exeter, a bell-founder in the reign of Henry VI
(1422–1461), and bears the inscription *Est michi collatum
istud nomen amatum* [It is my duty to give forth that beloved
name]. It is believed that the bell was brought from Cleeve
Abbey after the dissolution in 1538–9. Number one is the
most recent bell and is inscribed : ' I lead in the melodious
sound from hill and dale our pleasing notes resound ', this
was hung in 1896 and the names of the vicar and committee
for that year appear on the waist. The number two bell
inscribed ' Come let us sing for Church and King ' is dated
1723, as also is number four, which says ' Peace and good
neighbourhood '. The fifth bell gives the names of Sir Hugh
Windham, I. Wheddon, R. Gimlet, R. Hoopper, H. Morel,
and W. Holcomb, and is dated 1671 ; it is believed to have
been made at Bridgwater by Thomas Bailey, a well-known
bell-founder of Bridgwater during the sixteenth and seventeenth centuries. The sixth bell inscribed : ' I sound to
beid the sick repent in hope of life when breath is spent '
is dated 1668. At the time it was hung this bell was known
as the Passing Bell, it being then the custom to toll it when
a dying person was receiving sacrament so that those who
heard it could pray for the passing soul.

Items recorded in bishops' registers, old Somerset wills
and family histories throw a little light on the early history
of the church and give us an occasional picture of the people
concerned. In Bishop Drokensford's Register (Somerset
Record Society) we read that in the year 1310 Robert de
Halghtre was installed as Vicar of St. Decuman's, the Patron
being Canon de Gloster. A few years later, in the year 1319,

the Bishop, sitting judicially in St. Decuman's Church, pronounced the Rector of Ashe Regis canonically liable to pay a debt of £10 to one Rich de Luggare.

From the same source we find that in 1320 the Bishop announced that ' Robert, the Vicar of St. Decuman's, having represented the inadequacy of his portion for self and two chaplins ; We, finding the Rectory worth 24 Marks, 8s., the Vicarage 9 Marks, 4s., after consulting Rector and others, do now decree that the Vicar shall have the Vicar's house, all small tithes, tithes of four mills, and of dovecotes. All altilage (for augmentation) ; St. Decuman's Acre on north side of church, tithes of milk, butter, wool, small tithes of Donneford, with tithes of hay of free tenants of Donneford for horsemeat, of herbage, of churchyard, tithes of grain sown in curtilages (such augmented tithes valued at 8 Marks). Rector to have all other tithes, and 10/- from Vicar in aid of Clergy-taxes. Vicar to choose and remove chaplains and ministre (subordinates) but to swear them in fealty to Rector, and to keep books and ornaments in repair.'

Church robberies seem to have been quite common in medieval times and St. Decuman's apparently suffered with other churches from the attentions of thieves. The first recorded robbery occurred during the first year of the reign of Edward III, in 1327, when Gilbert the Walsh, or Welshman, was brought before the coroner and bailiffs of Bristol He was accused by Nicholas, the clerk of Watchet, of having with other unknown robbers broken into the church of Seyntdeycombe (St. Decuman's) and taken away a breviary, of the value of half a Mark (6s. 8d.) and a Psalter worth 3s. His pledges of prosecution were John of Kaynesham, merchant, John the Bond, Robert the Bond, and John of Wycombe. Gilbert was also accused by Nicholas of having, with other thieves, taken from the church at Watchet a silver chalice worth 13s. 4d., a silk bag to the value of 2s., in which the residue of the bread consecrated at Mass was placed, and a frontal for the Altar, valued at 3s.

In the year 1412 another robbery occurred, when we read that Richard Chelke, of St. Decuman's, was robbed of 7 Marks of 13s. 4d. each, two pieces of silver, six silver spoons, three mazers, two silk belts adorned with silver, and other goods to the value of £10, while on another occasion one Stacey Gegge was brought before Wm. de Montacute, Earl of Salisbury, and his colleagues, Justices of the Peace, for having stolen a chalice at St. Decuman's and goods to the value of forty shillings.

There are numerous entries in both Bishop Bekynton's and Bishop Ralph's Registers relating to the incumbents of St. Decuman's during the fifteenth and sixteenth centuries. Among them is one of 5th May, 1461, which is rather amusing ; it records the institution of Sir Nicholas Brown, chaplain, as perpetual vicar of the parish of St. Decuman, vacant by the resignation of Sir Robert Jamys, on the presentation of Master John Pope, canon of Wells and prebendary of St. Decuman's. Sir Nicholas appeared to the Bishop to be too simple in his knowledge of letters to have the cure of souls, and he was only admitted as an act of grace after he had sworn to study diligently until Tuesday in the consistory next after Easter, 1462, and to present himself then for re-examination by the Bishop, or the Bishop's chancellor or other commissary, and to resign his benefice if found still unfit.

Numerous bequests were made to the parish church and parishioners in medieval wills. A few interesting examples are as follows : In 1426, Thomas Shelforde, clerk of the Chancery, and canon of the Cathedral Church of Wells bequeathed ' . . . to the poor parishioners of my prebend of St. Decuman's 10 Marks '. In 1447 William Stevenes, Precentor of the Cathedral Church of Wells, bequeathed ' to

the fabric of the church of St. Decuman's 20s.' Joan
Sydenham, widow of Cannington, bequeathed 'to the newe
werke of the parish churche of Saynt Decuman 13s. 4d.'
in the year 1498, and again in the year 1555. Hugh Palmer
' fellowe of the newe college in Oxforde a long space ', left
' To poore folkes of the parishe of Watchett and Willyton
5s., the moste part thereof upon some one holidaye as two
such poore folke as shall be then present in the churche.'

Until about the middle of the nineteenth century the
living of St. Decuman's was known as a ' peculiar '. This
meant that the land, the great tithes, the buildings known
as Parsonage Farm, as well as the right of presentation to
the living, belonged to the prebend of St. Decuman's in
Wells Cathedral. It also entailed the right, through the
surrogate appointed by the prebendary, to prove wills and
to issue, independently of the Bishop, marriage licences.
The prebendary also had authority to lease the whole of
the great tithes, the lands, buildings, and the right of presentation to St. Decuman's for three lives. This was repeatedly
done for at least three centuries, the last instance being
when one of the Earls of Egremont paid no less than £10,000,
to Prebendary Watson, who was prebendary of the church
at that time, and who, so it is recorded, ' kept to his own use
the whole of that amount'.

The parish registers date from the year 1602. There
are few entries of any particular historical significance,
although the surnames and occupations of the people registered are of interest. The entries for the year 1603 give
several names which have now completely disappeared.
The names Dunborrow, Pym, Torrington and Hoole for
instance were quite common, while among the occupations
of this period that of husbandry was certainly the most
general. At the end of the eighteenth and early nineteenth
centuries the majority of males appeared to be engaged in

seafaring. Many of the present family-names of Watchet can be seen in seventeenth- and eighteenth-century entries : such names as Sully, Binding, Shorney, Nicholas, Wilkins, Webber, Besley, Hooper, and Chidgey appearing quite frequently.

The Chapel of the Holy Cross

The ' Chapell of the Holy Crosse of Wachet ' is mentioned several times in old records, and there is evidence that a chantry was founded in the chapel. Apparently certain small properties, including ' a messuage called Rood house ' and a ' Piscary called Rood Wear', formed an endowment. Among the documents in the Dunster Castle muniments room is a grant, dated 1370, by Geoffrey Loni, vicar of St. Decuman's, and John Ilond, to John Fitzours and his wife Joan in tail of lands between Watchet and Williton ' for the sustenance of a Chaplin celebrating in the Chapel of the Holy Cross, who in all his Masses shall pray for the souls of William Fitzours and Lucy his wife, John Fitzours and Joan his wife, and Annora and Joan their daughters [here follows a list of other members of the family] . . . and all faithful and departed.' The chapel was still in use in the reign of Edward VI, a document, dated 1549, is mentioned on page 64.

The actual site of the chapel is unknown, but it seems reasonable to assume that it was somewhere near the harbour, around which practically all the medieval town was situated.

St. Decuman's Charity

This Charity, the only one connected with St. Decuman's, and which until the 1939 war annually distributed blankets to the ' second poor ' of the parish, dates from the year 1582. A copy of the original document reads : ' This Indenture made in the sixteenth daie of Aprill in the fyve

and twenteth year of the Raigne of our Soveraigne Ladie
Elizabeth between Otewell Porter, son of John Porter of
Watchett, Glovier—and Thomas Joyner son of William
Joyner of Watchett, Husbandman.' Others mentioned in
the document are : George Gymlett, Watchett, Husbandman,
John Birkham, Yeoman, Silvester Bickham, Yeoman, John
Pyme, Wibble, Yeoman, John Jenkins, Streme, Husbandman,
William Bellamy, Streme, Weavor ; William Grynslade,
Williton, Husbandman, William Hancocke, Williton, Clothier,
John Moore, Williton, Husbandman, and John Dawe of
Bardon.

The income of the Charity was derived from the rent
of certain lands and properties which, to quote the document,
' The survivors heirs, shall pay yearly henceforth and forever
at the feaste of All Saintes to the church-wardens of St.
Decuman's.' Conditions laid down for the disbursement of
this money were as follows : ' for ye tyme beinge shall well
and trewlie yearlie for ever so often as the same shall come
to their handes Imploye the said Rente Issues fynes and
profits thereof or everie parte thereof coming and growinge
for of or by reason of the premises on the said reparacones
of the Pishe [Parish] Churche of St. Decuman's aforesaid
or els on ye setting foorthe of Solydieres to serve ye Queenes
Majestie in her Warres of Irelande or els where or els for ye
mayntenaunce of the Poore within the said Pishe or for
the defrayinge of anie other charge wherwith the inhabitants
of ye said Pishe are oughte or shalbe in anie sorte charged
or chargable by the Lawes of this Realme.' Among the
various plots of land mentioned are the following :—Gyllynge
Croft [Gillhams Croft ?], Magland, Loushill, ' one other half
acre thereof lieth by landshore in a common fielde called
Churche Waye ', another piece ' in a common fielde called
Wirylande ' [Wristland ?] and a portion of Culvercliffe.
Another property mentioned in the town is referred to as

' ye said Burgage lyeth in Watchett aforesaid in a Strete ther called Swyne Strete'.

The rents of some of these plots of land are still paid to the Charity, but in place of blankets, which had been distributed as long as the oldest inhabitant can remember, coal is now substituted.

The Dissolution and the Black Death

It is extremely unfortunate that there is an almost complete absence of historical record relating to Watchet during the period from the twelfth to the early part of the sixteenth century. We can only assume that the people of Watchet ploughed and harvested in their fields, sailed their little ships to the other ports of the Severn Sea, and worked at their local crafts and industries—as their fore-fathers had done before them. As far as we know they lived and worked in the same way, and under the same conditions, as the rest of the country during that period.

An event occurred in the sixteenth century which must have had some effect on the inhabitants of Watchet at that time, and though we have no actual documentary evidence from the town, the records from the immediate locality help a little to bridge the gap. At the time of the Dissolution of the monasteries, which took place from 1536 onwards, the Abbey of Clif [Cleeve Abbey] was receiving rent from land at Watchet. The Abbey was founded in 1188, and in all probability the land mentioned was granted to the monks by the de Moions, who are known to have made other benefactions to Cleeve. It is reasonable to suppose that there would have been close connexions between the monks of the Abbey and the people of the surrounding towns and villages of the district ; for instance, the evidence of the manufacture of tiles by the monks suggests a material link. During the period of the dissolution the King's Receiver,

Sir Thomas Arundell, who was touring Somerset, wrote to Thomas Cromwell : ' Riding down to Cornwall and passing the monastery of Clyffe, hearing much lamentation for the dissolution thereof, and a bruit in the country that the King, an you lordship's suit, had pardoned it, I sent to Mr Chancellor of the Augmentations to know whether to dissolve it . . . I beg on behalf of the honest gentlemen of that quarter that the house may stand. In it are seventeen priests of honest life who keep hospitality.' The Abbey appears to have been closed shortly afterwards despite the plea by Sir Thomas.

Another, and much more serious, event occurred in the middle of the fourteenth century. This was an outbreak of the dreaded plague known as the Black Death, the name given to a particularly violent form of bubonic plague which first made its appearance in England in 1348. During 1349 and 1350 it is estimated that one-third to one-half of the population of the country died, i.e. a total of between a million and a million and a half. The plague recurred on several occasions during the succeeding centuries ; and the last outbreak in 1665 is generally known as the Great Plague of London. Again we have no actual records of the plague at Watchet, but there is evidence that an earlier outbreak in 1550 was serious in the district, for the Parish Registers of Minehead, which begin in 1548, show that in the year 1550, while there were no burials at Minehead from April to September, fifty persons were buried in the month of October and twenty-one in November. It is reasonably certain from this that the plague also took its toll from Watchet at the same time ; very few, if any, towns or villages escaped its ravages, and the fact that seventy-one people died at Minehead during the outbreak shows what a high percentage of the population of that town had been stricken.

WATCHET, c. 1875

CHAPTER THREE

THE GROWTH OF WATCHET

The Armada and the Civil War

TOWARDS THE END of the sixteenth century there was
general apprehension at the constant threat of an invasion
from Spain and by the year 1580 local forces, or militia,
had been formed to defend each district. At this time
militia forces were raised by shires and called shire-levies.
Volunteers were encouraged, but if the desired numbers
were not forthcoming men were ' pressed ' into service.
This last method was certainly not beneficial for the Army,
as most towns and villages did their utmost to see that the
local ne'er-do-wells were taken by the recruiting officers.
There appears to have been a great deal of military activity
in Somerset during this period and Watchet was made one
of the six mustering places for the County. The Muster
Rolls of 1569 give the following list for the ' Tithing of
Wyllyton, Borough of Wachyt'.

Pikemen.	*Billmen.*	*Archers.*
Jno Dawe.	Robt Goodnowe.	Robt Sully.
Jno Uppington.	Robt Lange.	Jno Sully.
Jno Stephen.	Jno Lawham.	Thos Hole.
Geo Clowter.	Thos Cowche.	Humffry Bale.
Rich'd Towyll.	Geo Lewes.	Robt. Clowter.
Joset Foxxe.	Wm Campe.	Wm Sevyer.
	Rich'd Ellard.	Wm Tobrydge.
	Edw Gemlyt.	Wm Arnole.
	John Tayler.	Jno Heman.
	Barnard Emens.	Jno Trotte.
	Robt Wynter.	Jno Palmer.
	Jno Burde.	Samson Bowden.

Light Horseman.	*Billmen.*	*Archers.*
Harry Sully.	Abraham Pytte.	Harry Westlake.
	Nich Pytte.	Robt Herynge.
	John Sterell.	Wm Burde.
	Jno Durston.	Thos Cabell.
	Isott Sladd.	Jno Lawrens.
	John Ingram.	Hewe Lawrens.
	Roger Wallis.	Hugh Crosse.
	Wm Yowe.	
	Jno Selacke.	
	Hewe Burde.	

Armour.

One tithing corslet furnished.

John Saffye ⎫
John Tyler ⎭ a corslet.

John Trobrydge ⎫
John Seyer   ⎭ a corslet.

The importance of Watchet at that time can be assessed by comparison with other Somerset towns. The Tithing of Weston [Weston-super-Mare], for example, had one horseman, one pikeman, one archer, and four billmen, seven men in all compared to fifty-two men at Watchet.

The pikeman appears to have been the most important soldier on foot ; he carried a dagger and a broadsword, wore a complete corslet, and a helmet known as a burgonet. The billmen carried a halberd, which was a type of battle-axe with short points and long cutting edges attached to a stave about four feet nine inches long ; this was reckoned to be a particularly bloody weapon. These billmen furnished with corslets similar to the pikmen's were usually sent to the centre of the battle, often called ' the slaughter of the field '. The archers, armed with bows of yew, hazel, ash, or elm, also with sword and dagger, were still numerous and were regarded as the mainstay of an army. The term ' gonner ' appears in some of the Muster Rolls and such men were probably using the caliver and arquebus, the forerunner of the musket. These weapons gradually ousted the bow, for towards the end of the century the Privy

Council decreed that bows should be discontinued as weapons
of war from the year 1595.

Volunteers for the Navy appear to have been approached
in a much more subtle way than for the militia. The fishing
industry was considered to be of great importance at this
time, the chief reason, apparently, being that the fishermen
were excellent seamen and first-class material for the Navy.
Around 1580, as an encouragement to the fishermen, an
Act of Parliament of 1548 was renewed and enforced ordering
fish to be eaten by the general public on two days a week,
under penalty of fine. Though we have no local records of
naval recruiting during the period, it seems fairly certain
that some of the Watchet seamen were among the crews
of the ships that routed the Spanish Armada.

It is also interesting to note that just over two
centuries later, when England was threatened with invasion
by Napoleon, companies of ' Sea Fencibles ' were organized
by the Admiralty for guarding the coastline. These men
were also recruited from the sailors and fishermen and
records of 1803 show that there were thirty-nine ' Sea
Fencibles ' at Watchet, twenty-five at Minehead, and ten
at Porlock.

Although Watchet does not appear to have been deeply
involved in the Civil War, the struggle between King Charles
I and Parliament, under Cromwell, undoubtedly had its
effect on the town. The King's army, under the Marquess
of Hertford, marched into Somerset and took the Castles
of Taunton, Bridgwater, and Dunster in June, 1643. It
appears that the Royalists hoped to use the West Somerset
coasts and ports to bring in reinforcements from among
their supporters in South Wales. There is no doubt that
Watchet, which at that time was owned by Colonel Francis
Wyndham, an ardent royalist, was being used for that

purpose as the following curious note, from a life of Sir Robert Blake, shows :

' The King's party in Wales had sent a ship from thence to Watchet ; what its loading was is not mentioned, but the tide being at ebb, and the passage for horse being therefore commodious, Captain Popham's Troop, then on the coast, rode into the sea and attacked the men on board with brisk fire from their carbines, which soon did such execution among the Welch Gentry that they did their utmost to weigh and begone, but Popham's troopers plyed them so thick with their carbine shot, that to save their lives they surrendered the ship and themselves. The greatest rarity of all which is that a ship in the sea was taken by a Troop of Horse ; for the Troopers rode into the water, their horses Breast-deep, to come near enough to fire effectually at the enemy.'

Cromwell's forces under Blake besieged Taunton Castle and recaptured it in the spring of 1646. Shortly after this Blake, with a party of his troops, marched to Dunster, where, after a short siege, he forced the garrison to surrender. This episode appears to have brought the local participation in the Civil War to an end, and although the events mentioned appear to us to be unimportant as we look back on them from the twentieth century, they were no doubt very important, and exciting, to the people of Wachet at that time—for while many would have followed the local landowners in their support of the Royalist cause, there must have been quite a number who covertly sympathized with the revolutionaries of Parliament.

Early Industries

Scattered and fragmentary references from various historical sources to industry and trade at Watchet give one a picture of a little community which was fairly thriving in quite early times. Watchet's famous lime, for instance, was obviously in demand when the first Luttrell—Sir Hugh —came to Dunster Castle. For his household accounts for 1405 contain these entries : ' Paid for two quarters of lime bought at Wacet, together for 2d. for the carriage of the same 18d.', (for work being carried out on ' le Dongeon '). A translation of the Bailiff's Rolls for the Manor of Porlock states that at Michaelmas, 1419, the Bailiff, John Godde, paid ' For one quarter of plaster bought 2s. – 0d. To one man hired (to go) to Watchet to buy the aforesaid plaster, for his expenses 3d.' Accounts of the Manor of Wiveliscombe, 1474–5, also show that lime was purchased from Watchet for building a barn for the lord of the manor.

In the year 1429 the household accounts of Sir John Luttrell of Dunster show a payment to ' William Whevere of Whachet for weaving twenty-four yards of cloth, 2s.' In that century also the little town had a clockmaker, one John Smith, whose name and trade found their way on to parchment because he was summoned, in 1402, for a trespass, and was not to be found. During the reign of Henry VI a tyler, John Chamburleyne, was in business here ; he also was in trouble, on account of a debt of £20 he owed to a Bristol merchant. While an entry from the Trevelyan Papers giving expenses incurred at the funeral of John Trevelyan of Nettlecombe in the year 1492 reads ' to William Hurford of Watchet, for bred 3s. – 5d '.

Even from these scanty records we see that the burning of lime for plaster and building purposes, as well as the weaving of cloth, had been local industries for a period of at least five hundred years.

Defoe mentions the lime burning industry in his book, *A Tour through the Island of Great Britain*, which was published in 1724, in which he wrote : ' On this coast are vast quantities of rock, or rather pebble, which the sea at low water, leaves uncovered, from whence the neighbouring inhabitants fetch them on shore to an higher ground, and burn them into lime, for dressing their land, but it is more especially used in building, as no cement whatsoever is more lasting for *Jets d'Eaux*, Heads, Piers, and other masonry, that is to lie under water, in which position it runs up to a stone as hard as marble. The cliffs are stored with alabaster, which by the wash of the sea, falls down, and is conveyed from hence to Bristol, and other places on this shore, in great plenty. Neither should it be omitted that the inhabitants burn great quantities of sea-weed, to supply the glass makers at Bristol.'

The collecting and burning of sea-weed was also an industry that had been established centuries before it was mentioned by Defoe. In the records of Dunster Castle there is an agreement dated the 24th May, 1597, between George Luttrell of Dunster Castle and Robert Batten of Watchet in which the former agrees to let :

' All the oare now being or growing on that hereafter shall come to be within the ebbing or flowing of the sea in and upon the soil and inheritance of the said George Luttrell from the full sea mark unto the low-water mark extending from the bridge called Mouth Bridge unto the Warren House of the said George Luttrell commonly called or known by the name of the Whithouse from Midsummer next for 21 years at a rent of 26s. – 8d.'

Batten was forbidden by covenant from : ' burning any oare upon contrary winds that is to say upon any easterly wind, north, or north-east wind, whereby the smoke and noisome savour and smell of the said oare so burning may or shall be driven or carried toward the castle and house of the said George Luttrell, at Dunster aforesaid, or toward any of the lands of the said George Luttrell.' The boundaries mentioned are probably from Blue Anchor to Warren

Point at Minehead. The collecting and burning of seaweed was apparently an industry of importance for a very long period ; as nearly two centuries later, in 1766, an anonymous writer commenting on the shipping of Watchet states : ' They carry the ashes of sea-weed to supply the Glass-houses of Bristol, and great quantities of it are burnt for that purpose.'

The export of alabaster seems to have been an early and important industry. Gerard, writing in 1633, mentions :

' At this place in our tyme a Dutchman hath found out mynes of excellent alabaster, which they use much for tombs and chimney pieces. Its somewhat harder than ye Darbeshire alabaster, but for variety of mixtures and colours it passeth any I dare say of this Kingdom if not of others, for here you have some pure white, others white spotted with redd, white spotted with black, redd spotted with white and a perfect black spotted with white.'

A considerable trade developed later with the export of gypsum, which is an inferior form of alabaster. It was quarried from the cliffs between Watchet and Blue Anchor, and was shipped to Swansea and Bristol for the manufacture of plaster of paris. A certain amount was ground and used locally in the manufacture of some types of paper ; in fact, gypsum was used for this purpose until the 1914 war.

The fishing industry also played an important part in the economy of the port in the past. As early as the reign of Richard II (1381–1399) there were certain ponds, undoubtedly artificially made, known as ' le weres'. Owing to a trespass committed by the Earl of Devon who had taken them without Royal Licence, they passed back to the King who then leased them at 4s. 4d. a year. These ' weres ' are mentioned later in the Patent Rolls of Edward VI, 1549, where it states that ' for the sum of £265 – 15 – 6½ paid in the Augmentation by George Payne of Hutton,

Somerset, Gentleman', he was granted numerous possessions, chantries, etc., which included: 'the late chapel of Holy Cross of Wachet, and the plot of land in which that chapel stands, and also the messuage called Le Roodhowse and fishery called le Rood Were——.'

It is worth mentioning here that a few hundred yards north of the west pier, on what are known as the fishing grounds, there are still remains of a semicircular enclosure of large stones which could well be the foundation of one of these fishing ponds or 'weres'. Similar ponds have recently been examined by archaeologists in South Africa, where the natives used to construct identical semicircular enclosures. The walls were built without any form of mortar or cement, and as the water receded it filtered through the stones, leaving any fish within the enclosure high and dry. Such sea-water weirs are also well known in Ireland and some were in use until quite recent times.

Towards the close of the eighteenth century, in 1795, Billingsley, a government surveyor, mentions the salmon and, especially, the herring fishery of Porlock, Minehead and Watchet, as being considerable in extent. He suggested that the industry should be encouraged as much as possible to furnish employment during the winter months for the sailors who, during the summer months, were engaged in the limestone and coal trade. He pointed out that these men had an excellent knowledge of the Bristol Channel, that they were good pilots, and that the area would form a most valuable recruiting ground for the Royal Navy should the necessity arise.

By the middle of the last century sprat fishing was apparently the most valuable on the Somerset coast; it is on record that in November 1867 catches of sprats were larger than they had been for many years. A large quantity went to Bristol by rail, nearly a ton was sent to Wellington, and over three tons to Taunton, in addition to a considerable quantity sold in the neighbourhood. The estimated value of the sprat catches on this coast during a season, October to Christmas, was as much as £10,000, and it seems that it was a common sight in the cottages, months after the season was over, to see lines of sprats hanging from the rafters, while also stored in the house would be the inevitable barrel of salt herrings.

Salt was an indispensable commodity for fishing, agriculture, and domestic use from early times, and ' salting ' was the general method used to preserve both fish and meat. Its importance can be gauged by its frequent mention in the cargoes of vessels unloading at Watchet, and an interesting sidelight on this matter is given in a letter written by Thomas Windham of Kentsford, addressed to the Lord Chamberlain, Earl of Dorset, on 20th October, 1630, in which he states that one Derrick Popley of Bristol had sent a man called Yeoman to the various ports along ' the Severn on the English side ', to buy up all the salt he could get. At Barnstaple, Yeoman went from merchant to merchant pretending that he was going for a fishing voyage and in this way bought over 700 bushels. With a confederate named Jacob Andrewes of Bridgwater he also bought cargoes of two French ships at Watchet. As a result of this ' corner in salt ' the price had advanced from 4s. 8d. to 15s. 0d. a bushel, ' to the great grievance of all people and the ruin of many poor fishers for herring ', adds Thomas Windham.

Watchet Pottery

There is a strong local belief that pottery was once manufactured in Watchet and claims are still made that certain pieces are still in existence. This belief may have been strengthened by references to Watchet pottery made by Blackmore in his novel *Lorna Doone*. The writer has been unable to obtain any proof or historic reference of any kind to substantiate this claim, and as far as we know there are no traces of any old pottery kilns in the town, nor has any debris been found denoting the site of such kilns.   The writer believes that the legend is probably due to the use of the word *watchet* to describe the colour of certain pottery.   The origin of the word watchet to denote a colour is uncertain, but it is believed it may have come from a root of Old French.   The word has been used generally to denote a colour from the twelfth century onwards, but of recent years it has become obsolete.   It describes a rather dull hyacinth-like blue, very similar to the colour of the blue lias found at Watchet ; there is, however, no evidence to suggest that the origin of the colour-name watchet had any connexion with the place-name.   The following quotations give a few examples of the use of the word :

1386.   Chaucer, The Miller's Tale in the *Canterbury Tales*.

> ' Yclad he was ful smal and proprely
> All in a kirtel of lyght wachet.'

1589.   Hakluyt, *Voyages*.
' Mariners attired in wachet or skie-coloured clothe.'

1893.   J. Davidson, *Fleet Street Eclogues*.
' Wood-violets of watchet hue.'

The word is used by many other writers both in poetry and prose, including Shakespeare, Lyly, Camden, Collins, and Lamb.

Wool and Cloth

The wool trade and cloth industry in Britain was for several centuries second only in importance to agriculture. The early development of the industry in England was centred around London and East Anglia, in such towns as Lincoln, Colchester, Nottingham, and Oxford.   Later the industry gradually moved into the country districts, especially to the West of England, where a plentiful supply of running water was available to work the fulling mills. The importance of cloth manufacture can be assessed from the fact that during the lifetime of Chaucer the production of cloth was trebled and the quantity exported abroad was increased by over nine times. The value of the trade is shown by the protection given to it by both Edward II and Edward III ; during their reigns imports of foreign cloth into Britain were prohibited. The British had certain advantages over the people of other countries as sheep breeders and the high quality of their wool quickly gave them the commanding position in the European market.

Ample evidence of the importance of the industry in West Somerset in later times is afforded by the well-preserved and picturesque Yarn Market at Dunster ; and from an Act of Parliament of James I (early seventeenth century), we can obtain a good idea of the cloth made in this district. This Act states that ' every broad cloth, commonly called Tauntons, Bridgwaters, and Dunsters, made in the western part of Somersetshire, or elsewhere, or like making, shall contain, being thoroughly wet, between twelve and thirteen yards, and in breadth seven quarters of a yard at least, and being well scoured, thicked, milled, and fully dried, shall weigh thirty pounds the cloth at least.'

In the year 1714 there arose a dispute between some of the West Country merchants, probably clothiers, and the Luttrell family. Minehead being a Staple port, it was compulsory that all traders, importers and exporters of wool and cloth should have their goods weighed at Minehead town hall. There they were charged certain fees for weighing, as well as being assessed for taxes. Certain merchants of Tiverton, Taunton, and Minehead sponsored a petition to make Watchet the Staple port instead of Minehead. This, however, was strongly opposed by one Madam Luttrell, (who apparently at that time controlled the estate) and her trustees, supported by many tenants and the Mayors and Corporations of Taunton, Bridgwater, and Bristol. The result was that the petition was dismissed and Minehead remained the Staple port.

The idea of the Staple was to concentrate all wool and cloth exports at a few places thereby giving protection to traders against pirates and also to facilitate the collection of taxes.

The importance of the wool and cloth trade to Watchet in earlier years we can only surmise from the few scraps of evidence available. We have already seen that early in the fifteenth century one, William the Weaver, was making cloth at Watchet, and later on, as mentioned by the late W. H. P. Greswell in his book *The Land of Quantock*, a man named William Ferys of Wells, broke into the ' close ' of John Touker, or Tucker, in 1723, and carried away seven yards of cloth of ' Wachet ', worth 7s. 7d. It would not be wise to accept this reference as evidence that the cloth mentioned was manufactured at Watchet, despite the fact that Greswell writes, ' This is a local allusion of some interest. According to the explanation of some writers, Watchet had got to mean a colour of whitish blue. More probably it was a cloth manufactured at Watchet, and dyed with the juice of the Quantock whortleberry, still largely used as a dye.'

That there was a ' woollen manufactury ' well into the first half of the nineteenth century is shown by the reference in the letter to the Postmaster-General quoted on page 106. Although not yet having been able to determine the site, the writer has been informed that a ' fulling mill ' once stood on the little piece of land known as Silverside, which is situated between the church fields and the river. The fact that the meadow below, which runs down to the Mill Farm, is known as Rack Meadow, and was so called in the tithe apportionment list, is itself evidence of close association with the woollen industry. It will also be noticed that in the General Directory published in 1840 by the *Somerset County Gazette* (page 107) mention is made of Luke Organ, Mill-Puff manufacturer.

There appears to have been a cloth or blanket factory at Doniford for at least two centuries. The overseer's accounts of Dunster during the eighteenth century show that the inmates of the poorhouse spun yarn under the direction of Thomas Pulman of Doniford. They also show that Pulman took twenty per cent. profit on the work. The Doniford factory was situated at Swill Bridge, and it is interesting to note that the meadow adjoining was also known as Rack Meadow.

For several centuries the manufacture of cloth played a most important part in the lives and economy of the people of the countryside. Until the industrial revolution, most of the work was done in the home, the spinning being chiefly the work of the women and children, the weaving of the men. The clothier bought the wool and passed it to the spinners, weavers, fullers, dyers, etc., paying them all certain sums for each particular process ; the clothier was, in fact, as Trevelyan points out in his *English Social History*, the earliest capitalist organizer of industry. The trade left its mark on our speech and literature : such words, phrases, and metaphors as ' tease ', ' homespun ', ' spin a yarn', ' unravel a mystery ', ' web of life ', have come to us from the language of wool, as also such surnames as Weaver, Webber, Dyer, and Fuller. The calling of all unmarried women ' spinsters ' is believed by some authorities to have originated in the woollen trade.

Smuggling

Towards the end of the seventeenth century smuggling had assumed such serious proportions on the shores of the Bristol Channel that Charles II sent his Surveyor-General of Customs, Culliforde, to make a tour of inquiry of the district in the year 1682. His report makes both amusing and interesting reading, and it seems that one of the chief ' industries ' at this time was the ' running of goods ', in which almost everyone, from the lord of the manor downwards, was involved. Culliforde stated that the results of ' free trading ' in Watchet were such that ' from being beggars within this ten years the whole town has grown exceeding rich and now have as great an overseas trade as Minehead '. He also wrote, ' At Watchet it was found that several small vessels had no other business but that of running goods, and that the collector of customs there usually sat drinking with the masters of ships while gangs of men were unloading them.'

The collector of Customs, one William Dashwood, was evidently in league with the smugglers, for it is recorded that when he heard that the Surveyor-General was coming to Watchet he instructed his assistant Perry to swear that ' he was a very devil for strictness '. Unfortunately for Dashwood his assistant did not carry out his instructions, for, on 26th April, 1682, he made the following statement to Culliforde : ' About five months since came into ye harbour of Watchett the shipp Industry, Rob't Hooper Junr Master, loaden with salt, wine and brandy, part of which salt was entered and paid duties at the customs house of Mynehead, but the rest, with the wine and brandy, which was about 5 or 6 tuns, was run in the harbour, when at the same time Mr. Dashwood, the officer, was drinking with the master of the vessel at the signe of the Blew Anchor an alehouse in Watchett and this informant believes he was privy and consenting thereto.'

Another extract from Culliforde's report goes on to say : ' About four months since came into this harbour the shipp Adventure, Morgan Byneham master, of which vessel John Woolcotts of Tolland was part owner and was laden with wine, brandy, lynnen cloth, and salt. The salt entered and paid duty at Mynehead, but the wine, brandy and cloth all run and was a very considerable parcell for there was not lesse than 30 men at worke between two and three hours delivering the same and all that while Mr. Dashwood was drinking sack with the master at the Shipp tavern and was privy and consenting to the same which this Informant knows to be true for that the same Mr. Dashwood spoak to this Informant to deny his being in the house, for fear one Ambrose Webber should inform against him, the said Webber having just before endeavoured to disturb the persons that were running the said goods by setting his dogg at them at which action the said Mr. Dashwood was very angry and called him damned rogue for endeavouring to disturb the persons that were running the said goods.'

Available evidence proves that the Watchet smugglers did not give up their profitable business without a struggle ; for instance, when some of the King's officers tried to board the *Industry* to prevent her from sailing without paying duty, Hooper and his crew drew swords and drove off the customs men and sailed away. The outcome of Culliforde's investigations was that Dashwood was suspended and Perry was provisionally appointed in his place. Culliforde concluded his report on Watchet with these words : ' And for as much as the said Mr. Perry for making the discovery and doeing the king service, has begotten himselfe a generall hatred throughout the Town of Watchett (which belongs to Sir William. Windham who patronizes them in all their

actings) and for that the said Perry is a person well qualified
for the said service, but I cannot but humbly offer he may
be established in the room of William Dashwood suspended.'

Though Perry may have been a more zealous official
than his predecessor, it is extremely doubtful if he was
completely successful in preventing the ' running of goods '.
The fact is that this was considered quite a legitimate
business, in which the sailors, traders, and lord of the manor
all had a hand.   There were probably many accomplices
among the townsfolk and there must have been many cellars
and out-of-the-way hiding places around Swain Street and
Market Street where contraband goods and liquor were
hidden.

The Court Leet

When William of Normandy conquered England he
already found a large part of the population settled in towns
and boroughs, working under a system of local government.
The ' free ' inhabitants met several times a year to settle
and to deal with matters of local importance at a borough-
moot or port-moot.   At this meeting a chief officer was
elected, usually called a Port Reeve, and his duties were to
collect general dues or taxes, to preside over the local court,
and to represent the townsmen should any difference arise
between them and the King.   Records of these moots or
courts were kept in many parts of England from the
thirteenth century onwards, and it is from these records
that historians have obtained a great deal of our present
detailed knowledge of the social structure and conditions
of the Middle Ages.

A Court Leet is still held annually in Watchet, but
whereas to-day it is only a token court, in the past it was
an authoritative court in which all matters of local importance were settled.   The date of the earliest records of the

Watchet Court Leet is the year 1620, though there is little doubt that the court was in existence centuries before. In fact, the high importance of Watchet in Saxon times makes it fairly conclusive that its status warranted a court-moot at that period. The records show that the Watchet court was held twice a year until 1659, since which date one court a year has been held in the month of October.

The court was summoned some days before it was due to meet, and the Bailiff issued notices to fifteen townsmen as follows :

' Town and Borough of Watchet, in the county of Somerset. I hereby summon and warn you to appear at the Court Leet with a view of Frankpledge of . . . [the name of the lord of the manor at the time] at the Bell Inn, within the said Town and Borough, on . . . instant, by twelve oclock in the forenoon precisely, to serve our Soverign Lord the King and the Lord of the said Leet, and herein fail not at your peril.'

At the opening of the court, the jury answered to their names, and any absentees, after their names had been called three times, were fined six shillings and eightpence at the next court. The office of Foreman was taken in turn by each of the jurors. The following oath was then administered to him by the president :

' You as foreman of this inquest, shall enquire and true presentment make of all such things as shall be given you in charge. The King's Counsel, your own, and your fellows you shall well and truly keep. You shall present nothing out of hatred or malice, nor shall you conceal anything out of fear, favour or affection, but in all things you shall well and truly present, as the same shall come to your knowledge, according to the best of your skill and judgement. So help you God.'

The remainder of the jury then took the oath, four at a time to begin with, followed by the Portreeve, who was elected annually.

Here is a copy of the proceedings of the Court Leet held at the Bell Inn on the 27th of October, 1733 : I give this as being an example typical of the life of the period :

Watchett
Burroughs

The presentments of the Jury of the Court Leet holdin and for the Burrough of Watchett aforesaid in the name and on behalf of Sir. Wm. Wyndham Bar. Lord of the said Leet and Burrough on Saturday the Twenty Seventh Day of October in the Seventh Year of King George the Second and in the Year of our Lord God 1773.

Names of Jury.

Richard Luckes.	Foreman.
John Danniell	John Cooch
Amos Hooper	John Westron
John Good	Sam Besley
Ben Williams	Wm Webber
Richard Luckes Jnr	Nath Besley
Thomas Chidsey	Wm Tipling

First   We present Mr. Richard Luckes to be Port Reeve of the Burrough of Watchett for the year ensuing............ ....Sworn in Court.

Also   We present Wm Webber and Wm Tipling to do the office of Petty Constables for the Burrough of Watchett for the year ensuing........................Sworn.

Also   We present Gyles Browning and Isaat Westron to be Bread Weighers for the Town and Burrough of Watchett for the ensuing year.......................

Also   We present John Stone and John Jenkins to be Ale Tasters in and for the Town and Burrough of Watchett for the year ensuing.......................Sworn.

Also   We present the Want of a Cucking Stoole and Pillory and that the same ought to be Erected at the charge of the Lord of the Manor.

Also   We continue John Nicholas to be Street Keeper for the year ensuing.

Also   We present the Winnowing of Corn in the Streets of Watchett to be a Nusance to the Inhabitants of the Town and that a penalty of Five Shillings be Laid upon each and every person that shall do the same for the Future for every Offence.

Also   We present the Ship Loading to the Key to be out of Repair.

Also We present the Sifting of Ashes in the Streets of Watchett
to be a Nusance to the Inhabitants of the Town and
that a Penalty of One Shilling be Laid and Levyed upon
Every person that shall be Guilty of the Like Offence
for the Future.

Gyles Browning one of the persons Nominated to be a
Bread Weigher for the year ensuing not coming into Court
to be Sworn and also John Stone one of the Ale Tasters the
Jury did order that the said Gyles Browning and John Stone
be Sworn before a Justice of the Peace within Tenn Days after
this Court under the Penalty of Forty Shillings each of them
making Default.

There are many items from the Court Leet proceedings
which are very informative and give us a good insight into
the life of the town and the characters of its inhabitants
during the past few centuries. The following extract, for
example, from the records of the year 1743 shows the
importance of the fishing industry and also how severe the
judgment of the Court could be on what they regarded as
Sabbath-breaking :

' We present all persons having out Netts on Sundays
in order to fish or be spread for Fishing before Six O Clock
Eivoning to be amerised Ten Shillings for every offence.'
(An Amercement was a fine imposed by a Court.)

The state of the roads and footpaths were often under
discussion. In the records of 1747 we read : ' We present
the Town Bridge to be much out of repair.' ' We present
the Streets to be much out of repair.' ' We present the
foot road Leading to Almascroft and Five Acres.' ' We
present the road from the Town Bridge to Damson Bridge
to be out of repair.'

The Town Bridge mentioned must have been in the
same situation as the existing bridge at the end of Market
Street, which would have been the centre of the town at
this time ; Damson Bridge was probably a smaller bridge
over the river near the present bridge at Waterloo Cottages.

The foot-road leading to Almascroft and Five Acres was undoubtedly what is now known as Goviers Lane.

One of the older inhabitants of Watchet informed the writer that he had been told many years previously by old people that a stream once ran through Swain Street, and this is confirmed by an entry in the records of the year 1812, which reads : ' We present the Covering Stones of the Drain through Watchet Street to be of bad materials and the same ought to be kept in better repair by the Surveyor of the Highways.' The condition of the streets was constantly mentioned over a long period ; evidently the inhabitants caused the Jurors of the Court Leet a great deal of bother, and they made, apparently, quite a regular practice of sifting ashes, and winnowing corn, in the streets. This was brought up time and time again in the records, and although on each occasion fines were imposed the people of Watchet persisted in these offences ; in addition, mention is also made of folk allowing their pigs and other animals to run around in the streets. Another offence is one recorded in the year 1711 where we read : ' We present John Perrott for a Nusance for emptying out of Chamber Pots into the street.'

Another source of annoyance to the court was the practice of making dung heaps in the streets, an extract from the records of 17th October, 1717, reads : ' We further Present that if any Inhabitants or House keeper leaves any Dung in the Streets above five Days after Notice Given to them by the Streete Keeper to Remove the same Such Dung shall be forfieted by ye Streete Keeper itt being the Ancient Custom of the Burrough so to be.'

Some of the extracts give us then an idea of the un-satisfactory state of the streets in the town ; the sifting of ashes, the winnowing of corn, to say nothing of the running of pigs and the emptying of sewage, must have made the roads very much like farmyards, especially in wet weather. The repeated references to the winnowing of corn point to the fact that there were then a number of farms in the town. As we have already seen, this was typical of the medieval period, and it seems quite likely that the actual layout of Watchet a century and a half ago had altered very little from that of the Middle Ages. It is interesting to note that even as late as the early part of the present century no less than four farms were occupied right inside the town : that of Mr. John Date was behind the present Post Office, which building was the farmhouse ; Mr. Llewellyn Hole's was at the top of Swain Street, the farmyard being on the site of the present-day Van Heusen shirt factory ; another farmyard was on the site of the Conquest Cinema, Esplanade House being the farmhouse ; and the fourth farm, the Mill Farm, is still in existence.

Occasional entries in the records give us some idea of the methods of trading and reminders of past industries. For example, one item in the records of 29th October, 1725, shows us that the butchers from the surrounding country-side came to Watchet on market days; the entry reads: ' We Present that all the Butchers horses who Comes to the Market and Stand in the Streat above half an hower ought to be putt into ye Pound by ye Streat keeper and that such Butchers who Suffer there horses to Stand in ye Streats longer than ye time above incautioned ought to pay four Pence for Each horse.' Two items connected with the manufacture of cloth occur in the records of 1728 and 1745. The first states : ' We Present yt ye Letting Dielicker [dye liquor] into ye River is a Nusence to ye Inhabitants.' The second says : ' We Present the Heirs of Mr. Richard Luckis to has Luckis Land and ye Dyhouse for ye life of John Luckis.'

The court was entitled to give judgement and mete out punishment for petty crimes, breaches of contract, and breaches of assize : that is the established standard of measure for wheat and coal, and also the established quality of bread and beer. In the year 1712 the court considered that the Port Reeve Bushel was not a true measure owing to it being only sixty quarts whereas it should have been ' sixty five Winchester quarts—as the ancient custom of the Burrough Requires '. An entry in the records of 12th October, 1728, shows that this measure was again increased to ' Sixteene gallans and two Quarts ' thus making the Port Reeve bushel sixty-six quarts.

Measures for the sale of coal were also discussed and amended at the court proceedings ; a detailed example comes from the records of 1712 and is entered thus : ' Wee Present all the Coal pecks by which Coal is sold in this Burrough to be too little for whereas the said pecks do Containe now but Nine Winchester quarts sack Wee present that they ought to Containe Ten quarts according to the Ancient Custom of the said Burrough. Wee Present that a new peck containing Ten quarts be made within Ten Dayes after the Date hereof and that all Sellers of Coal and Culme do provide themselves with pecks containing Ten quarts sacks within the time above limited by which to Sell their Coal and Culme upon the penalty of five pounds sack person making Default.'

The Steward of the Lord of the Manor who presided over the Court Leet appears to have been vested with full judicial powers over the members of the court and an instance of a steward exercising this right is given in the year 1746 ; his summing-up is entered thus : ' Edward Escott and John Slocombe Being Sworn of the Jury and Homage fought before the Presentment was delivered in and upon the Votes of the Jury viz'd three of 'em the rest

not seeing the Battery John Slocombe was the agressor
and in my Judicial Capacity I fine him Six Shillings and
Eight Pence.'

Below appears the voting of the three jurors who
witnessed the assault :

Edward Escott Struck first   John Slocombe Struck first

I

I

I

The Constables, too, held much more important and
responsible posts than would appear from a casual reading
of the records. In addition to their duties of keeping the
peace they were responsible for taking people to prison,
acting as rate-collectors, procuring warrants, and attending
courts. The following is a copy of the Constables' accounts
for the year 1729, when Joseph Holmes and John Nicholas
were Constables :

'The Cunstables acoo^{tt}
Charges on Ann Slocomb and ffamily to std.

Paid for thire Mittimis*	8 – 0
Paid ye gardsman Joseph Davis	4 – 0
Paid Matthew Davis	4 – 0
Paid John Bray	4 – 0
Paid Jno Attiwell	1 – 6
Paid Wm Williams	1 – 6
Paid Christopher Webber	1 – 6
Paid Mrs. Dagg for house Charges	5 – 4
Paid George Thorn	1 – 0
Paid att Yard mill ye house Charges	13 – 0
Paid ye County Money	2 – 3¾
Paid for making and Writing ye Borrow Rate	2 – 0
Paid for men and horses to Carry Slocombe and her ffamily to prison	3 – 14 – 4
Paid Mrs Dagg for house Charges	8 – 5
Paid Jno Gimletts house Charges	2 – 2
James Holtts Charges Carrying him to prison Paid Jno Skinner house Charges	3 – 9
Paid for ye Mittimis	1 – 0

* A warrant committing a person to prison.

Paid ye gardsman to Carry him to prison	10 – 0
Charges on ye Rode	7 – 0
Charges to Carry Matt Davis to prison	
Paid Jno Wathing house Charges	4 – 9
Charges to Crocomb and from Crocomb to prison	9 – 2
Paid 4 gardsmen on ye same aco't	7 – 0
Paid for ye mittimis	1 – 0
Charges att Yard mill Returning ye Vittelrest†	1 – 10
Charges on Matt Davis Carring him before Sir John Trivoyliyan on ye Sute of Margaret ffort	7 – 6
Paid Mr Wakefield for an Oath	1 – 0
Paid ye Marshollse Money	1 – 6¼
ffor Returning ye freholders Warrant	1 – 0
Paid for ye Kings proclamation	6

                                              9 – 10 – 1½

Collected by 8 Borrough rates at   1 – 7 – 8½
                                                   8

Totall of ye 8 rates is   11 – 1 – 8
Due to be paid ye Constable ye sum of   1– 11 – 6¼
Collected from Jno Slocomb   2 – 0

                                              1 – 13 – 6¼

† Bins or barrels in which the ground flour for breadmaking (the victuals) were brought from the mill to the prison.

The Court Leet, despite the fact that it was under the control of the Lord of the Manor's Steward, enabled its members to exercise a measure of independence. The members of the court had certain rights which they jealously guarded, and they were not slow to threaten the Lord of the Manor with a fine if he neglected any communal responsibility, as the records of the Watchet Court Leet show on numerous occasions. Members were often poor and sometimes unable to sign their names, according to the records; despite this their votes as judges of the Court were final, and guided by the 'ancient customs of the Borrough' they were often able to check any tendency on the part of the landlord to tyrannize over village or township.

CHAPTER FOUR

COMMERCE AND PEOPLE

The Harbour

FROM THE preceding chapter it will have been observed
that the harbour was of the greatest importance to Watchet
from very early times, although we have as yet little factual
evidence about either its structure or its use in the Saxon
and medieval periods. The accounts of the Danish raids
on the town given earlier (page 22) suggest that Watchet
must have been a convenient landing-place or port, and
from Ireland comes some very interesting evidence suggesting
either trading connexions or raids. The first coins to be
struck in Ireland were issued under the authority of Sihtric
III, a Norse King of Dublin, somewhere around A.D. 1000.
In the collection of early Irish coinage at the National
Museum of Ireland in Dublin there are two coins of Sihtric
III bearing on the reverse the legend *Sigeric—Peced*. This
being the name of the Watchet moneyer Sigeric and the
town of Watchet. Several writers in the past have assumed
from this that the Norse king actually minted money at
Watchet. Worsaae, in his book *The Danes and Norwegians
in England, Scotland and Ireland*, states that ' This king
was more than once driven into exile, and as he used this
mint as well as others in England, must have made Watchet
his port of refuge.' From enquiries the writer has made
it would appear that such an assumption is quite incorrect ;
officials of both the British Museum and the National
Museum of Ireland hold the opinion that the coins were
made in Dublin and were slavishly copied from coins of

Æthelred II minted in Watchet, which had probably been acquired either as a result of trade with the inhabitants or in raids made upon them by the Norse king.

That there was some sort of substantial construction as early as the reign of Henry VIII is suggested by a quaint plan of the Bristol Channel, preserved among the Cottonian MSS. in the British Museum, which shows proposed coastal defences. The port of ' Watchatte ' is depicted as having a ' were', evidently of timber, which shelters three vessels. One of these might be taken to represent the ' Margrett of Watchet', Philip Moore, master, which is mentioned in a list of shipping noted at Bridgwater in 1519.

Later maps of Watchet show a breakwater built on the western side of the harbour ; it was probably composed of wooden piles with a stone core, known as the Cobb type of harbour. The same type of harbour existed in all probability for centuries, and it is evident that then, as now, the structure of the breakwater occasionally suffered great damage as a result of gales.

What information we have of such calamities from medieval times comes chiefly from ecclesiastical ' briefs', a form of appeal which was circulated to various churches. The earliest appeal on behalf of Watchet is recorded in Bishop Bekynton's Register, and was issued on the 28th June, 1458. This ' Exhortation and injunction to all ecclesiastics of the diocese ' reads ' inasmuch as the port which was at one time in the parish of Wagget is well nigh demolished and utterly destroyed by storms, owing to lack of due maintenance of the walls and other buildings thereof, and the inhabitants of the said parish and the ajacent parts are striving to the best of their ability to build up and repair the same with great labour and at great expense, but their means are not sufficient to complete so costly a work without the charitable alms of the faithful '.

Two centuries later in the winter of 1658–1659, heavy gales had again severely damaged the harbour, for in the records of the old London church of St. Christopher-le-Stocks (which was pulled down in 1780–81, to make room for extensions to the Bank of England) is the following entry : ' 1660 June ye 16th. Collected towards ye repaire of ye Peere and Harbour of Watchplatt in ye County of Somerset ye summe of twenty-two shillings.' In the following year, 1661, a collection was also made at St. Margaret's Church, Westminster, ' towards the making good of a defense against the water in the towne and burrow of Watchett in our County of Somersettsheere.'

Collections were also made in the West Riding of Yorkshire, at Dursley, and Deerhurst in Gloucestershire, Hopton Castle in Shropshire, and Compton Bishop in Somerset. In one or two of these appeals the extent of the damage is given as £3,000.

There are probably many more records of funds raised for the same purpose hidden away in parish registers, but these examples are sufficient to show that the harbour disasters of the past half-century are nothing new for the people of Watchet.

Again in the year 1707 the ' inhabitants, freeholders, and lords of Watchet ' petitioned Parliament to sanction a by-law allowing them to lay a duty upon all sorts of goods imported or exported from the harbour. The object of raising revenue in this way was to have funds available to meet such a contingency as had recently arisen when ' by the violence of the sea the said town and navigation there is almost lost, their quay being quite thrown down to the great prejudice of Her Majesty's Customs, the loss of several ships sailing to Bristol and Bridgwater, and the utmost peril of ruining the remaining part of Watchet town.'

Several Acts of Parliament have been made in connexion with Watchet harbour from the reign of Queen
Anne onwards. The first appears to have been passed in
the sixth year of that Queen's reign, 1708, and another Act
was passed in 1712. A further Act was passed in the seventh
year of the reign of George I, 1721, and the following
extracts from this document are of interest regarding certain
structural details and also for the information relating to
the levying of dues and the boundaries of the port.

> WHEREAS by an Act of Parliament made and passed in
> the sixth year of the reign of Her late Majesty Queen Anne,
> Intituled, An Act for repairing the Harbour and Key of
> Watchett in the County of Somerset, It was Enacted, that
> from and after the Five and twentieth Day of March, One
> Thousand seven hundred and eight, for the Term of One and
> twenty Years and from thence to the End of the then next
> Session of Parliament, there should be paid the several Rates
> and Duties in the said Act mentioned and expressed, for all
> Goods and Merchandizes exported, shipped, or laden, or
> imported landed or discharged, at or within the said Harbour
> or Key ; . . . and after the Expiration of the said Term of
> One and Twenty years, One half of the said Rates and Duties
> by the said Act granted . . . were to continue to be collected
> for ever, in order for the raising a sufficient Stock and Supply
> for the keeping the said Harbour and Key in good Repair ;
> and whereas it is found by Experience, that when the said
> Key was rebuilt and repaired, the same was built much too
> low, and not extended to a sufficient length to preserve the
> Town of Watchett aforesaid, and the Ships and Vessels riding
> in the said Harbour, from the Rage and Violence of the Sea,
> and it is absolutely necessary that the said Key should be
> raised much higher than it is at present . . . [the Act continues]
> . . . It is Enacted, that all goods shipped or discharged at a
> Place called the Blew Anchor or Cleave Steps, or other Places
> ajoining to the said Harbour and Key of Watchett, should be
> chargeable with the Duties as if the Goods had been shipped
> or discharged within the said Harbour or Key of Watchett.

For something like three centuries, at any rate, Watchet
appears to have had a considerable fleet of coasting vessels
plying up and down the Bristol Channel, to Ireland, as
well as to Liverpool, London, and other British ports.
Some of the larger vessels also traded to Antwerp, Rotter-
dam and other Continental ports. The earliest record of

Watchet vessels that I have been able to trace is that given
by Hancock in his *History of Minehead*, in which he records
that the following ships called at Minehead either with or
to load cargo, during the year 1647. The particulars were
taken from the accounts of Minehead port :

George. of Watchett—bound for Wales.
Hart.   ,,   ,,
Grace. ,,   ,,
Speedwell.   Rob. Hooper (captain ?)
The Costley.
The Black Boule.   Dashwood (owner ?)
Jenkin. of Watchett (14 pigs out of Tinby)
Garland. ,,   ,,   George Vey. (captain ?)

In the year 1673, during the reign of Charles II, Watchet
had quite an imposing fleet of vessels for we read that ' the
Endeavour of Watchet, John Smith, Master, took 350 bushels
of peas to Barnstaple, the *Guift*, George Priest, Master, took
400 winchesters of wheat, 100 bushels of oats, 60 bushels
of peas, 21 barrels of English fish and herrings, one grose
of ox bowes, and one packe of woollen cloth to Bristol.
The *Truelove* of Watchet, Robert Hooper, Master, was
laden with 60 bushels of peas, 4 barrels of herrings, and 5
packs of woollen cloth. The *Phoenix*, William Washer,
Master, was laden with 150 bushels of wheat, 2 packs of
thrums, 4 fardels of canvas, 53 balkes of stones, and one
hogshead of tobacco containing 300 pounds. The *May-
flower*, Robert Hooper, Master, with 14 chalders of coals
from London, the *Exchange*, Humphrey Hooper, Master,
with 20 chalders of coals from Neath, the *George* of Watchet,
Robert Hooper, Master, with 14 chalders of coals, the
Marygold, Humphrey Hooper, Master, with 24 chalders of
coals also entered or left the harbour of Watchet this year.'

Apparently both Robert and Humphrey Hooper liked
a change of ships for we find one commanding three and

the other two vessels during the year.   The various items
of cargo are extremely interesting, and show the importance
of agriculture, the wool trade, and fishing.   Coal seems to
have been imported in considerable quantity for the period,
from London as well as South Wales.   A chalder or chaldron
was a measure of coal containing from thirty-two to thirty-
six bushels, and a winchester was the old form of bushel
which was used generally for wheat.   Another list of
Watchet ships and their owners is given by Hancock for
the year 1790:

VESSEL.	OWNER.	VESSEL.	OWNER.
Good Intent.	John Hurley.	*Friends Increase.*	Thomas Jenkins.
Molly.	George Union.	*Prosper.*	Francis Jenkins.
Brothers.	Richard Luckes.	*Shepherdine.*	David Stephens.
Social Friends.	William Hole.	*Susanna.*	Richard Web.
Ann.	William Crocker.	*Windham.*	John Lucas.

That the merchants and ship-owners of Watchet and
district were ready to accept such new and revolutionary
innovations as steamships is clearly shown by an existing
poster summoning a public meeting at Williton in 1834.
It is quoted in full:

THE PUBLIC
are respectfully informed that
A GENERAL MEETING
will be held

at the Wyndham Hotel, in Williton, on Saturday
the 29th Day of March instant, at 11 o'Clock in
the forenoon, for the purpose of considering the
propriety of putting a

STEAM VESSEL
on the Coasting Trade Between
BRISTOL, WATCHET, and MINEHEAD,

And if the measure should be found practicable, a
Trading Company will be formed, and such further
steps taken as shall be then determined on for
carrying it into immediate effect.   In the meantime,
information on the subject will be received or
given by

Thomas Hawkes,
Land Agent etc., Williton.

Dated 19th March, 1834.

Whitehorn, Printer & Bookbinder,
Watchet.

The heyday of Watchet's maritime prosperity was undoubtedly the later half of the nineteenth century, when the rapid expansion of industry and commerce had its effect in practically every port in the country. An estimate of the considerable trade both in and out of Watchet harbour at this period can be gained from the following figures :

YEAR	NO. OF VESSELS INWARDS	REG. TONS	NO. OF VESSELS OUTWARDS	REVENUE
1860	445	13,954	446	£387
1861	524	19,818	520	£530
1862	557	22,759	553	£688

Imports of coal during the three years were 10,412, 12,344, and 13,030 tons respectively. Coal discharged at Quantoxhead, Lilstock, St. Audries, and Blue Anchor are included in these figures for the first two years.

The late Mr. A. B. L. Pearse, of Watchet, with the assistance of the late Captain S. Allen, compiled a list of all the vessels of Watchet over a period of the past seventy-five years. Presented to the Watchet Urban District Council by Mr. Pearse in 1932, it now hangs in the council chamber. Details of one hundred and twenty-six sailing vessels are given in the list, which ranges from small ' smacks ' of just over twenty tons to large schooners up to three hundred tons. Two of the ships listed were built locally ; the largest, the *Star of the West*, a schooner of one hundred and forty tons, was launched, the writer understands, about the middle of the century from the site on which the Library (formerly the Lifeboat house) now stands.

Such a large number of small vessels trading in and out of Watchet often meant a heavy toll in both ships and the men that manned them. This is tragically shown by an extract from the *West Somerset Free Press* of 10th February, 1883. ' Watchet has had a particularly unfortunate experience with its shipping, the present year having opened very disastrously. It is but a few weeks ago that the *Martha* went down, with the loss of four men. Last week we had to record the loss of the *Kelso* and her crew, and now comes the news of the *Taunton Packet*. This is in addition to minor casualties and vessels reported missing. Since the great gale of October, 1859, no less than twenty-six vessels hailing from Watchet have been totally wrecked with the loss of twenty-seven men.'

Passenger services by boat to Bristol and South Wales must have been an old-established form of communication for centuries. The earliest records the writer has been able to trace are of the year 1830, when sailings were made to Bristol every fortnight by the *Union Packet* (Thomas Press, Master) and by the *Friendship* (John Price, Master). Sailings were also made to Newport and Swansea by the *Watchet Trader, The Friends, Ceres, Moderator*, and the *Love*. A few years later came the 'Steam Packets'; the first on this coast seems to have been the *Lady Charlotte* of Bristol, described at the time as ' the new and fast-going steam packet, with two engines, 30 h.p. each '. This boat sailed from Bristol to Minehead on 23rd July, 1837, the fares being 6/6 after cabin, 4/6 fore cabin. Apparently it did not call at Watchet.

By the middle of the century ' Marine Excursions ', as they were advertised, had been firmly established ; in fact on one trip in 1850 it is recorded that ' six persons were drowned through wanton carelessness in embarking at Watchet during a pleasure trip by the Neath Abbey.' The files of the *West Somerset Free Press* contain numerous advertisements of sailings, from the year 1860 onwards.

PLATE III

MOUNT PLEASANT BEFORE THE RAILWAY STATION WAS BUILT, SHOWING ROPEWALK (UNDER TREES) 1850's

PLATE IV

THE CROSS IN THE 1850's.   FARM BUILDINGS RIGHT FOREGROUND

We read that in August of that year ' *The Lord Beresford,* (H. Pockett, Swansea, Commander), fast and commodious pleasure steamer, sailed from Watchet to Bristol ', and again on 1st September, ' Pockett's Boat, *Prince of Wales,* from Watchet to Ilfracombe.   Fares, best cabin 4/6, fore cabin 3/-.' For some time after this there appears to have been a boom in pleasure cruises, one of the pioneers, the founder of ' Date's Marine Excursions ', being Richard Stoate Date, who died at Cardiff in 1899.   Mr. Date chartered boats which were used as tugs in the winter and   converted to passenger boats during the summer season.   The popularity of these trips is shown by the fact that sometimes no less than three boats left Watchet on the same morning. Such an instance was on 4th August, 1863, when the *Geo. P. Bidder,* the *Iron Duke,* and the *Pilot* all left   for Ilfracombe.

The opening of the railway from Taunton to Watchet had a most stimulating effect on the ' marine excursion ' business, for we read that on 1st September, 1863, a special train arrived at Watchet from Taunton ' containing a thousand people bent on cruising from Watchet to North Devon.' On this occasion the *Iron Duke* failed to appear, and while about five hundred people were literally packed into the *Pilot* and the *Geo. P. Bidder,* the remainder had to be content with spending the day at Watchet.   On another occasion, in 1866, we read that ' one of Date's steamboat excursions brought three hundred people from Bristol on Whit-Monday.   Their landing caused some little amusement, for being too late to find water enough to enter the harbour, the passengers were brought ashore, some in boats, others in carts, and not a few on the backs of men.   Some in their eagerness to get ashore were thoroughly drenched, others found themselves too deep in mud to be comfortable.'

Two unusual news items of sailings in June, 1867, show that Captain Wedlake's *Patriot* ran from Watchet and from Sir Peregrine Acland's pier at Lilstock, to Cardiff, and that Mr. J. Lockyer, of Minehead, another promoter ot marine trips, ran ' the new fast-sailing *Usk* ', from Minehead, Watchet, and Lilstock to Avonmouth. On this trip ' the excellent Stowey Brass Band, under the leadership of Mr. Glover ' was engaged. Bands were often engaged for these excursions, and among the bands mentioned, in addition to the above, were the Taunton Band of Hope Fife and Drum Band and the Monksilver Band. The last band played a valiant part on an eventful trip in August, 1861, when the *Iron Duke* was returning from Bristol to Watchet. The wind was dead against the vessel and it was impossible to make Watchet before midnight, by which time the tide was out and the vessel was compelled to anchor in Blue Anchor Bay. Here the passengers spent a most uncomfortable night, though cheered by the music of the Monksilver Band until daybreak, when the *Iron Duke* raised anchor and steamed to Minehead, where the weary passengers were relieved to get ashore.

These converted boats were later superseded by boats of the Red Funnel and White Funnel fleets. Specially built for passenger services, they became a regular feature of summer traffic in the Bristol Channel. The Red Funnel Fleet ceased to operate in the early years of the present century, but Messrs. Campbell's White Funnel Fleet still carry many thousands of people over the waters of the Severn Sea during the summer season, but, unfortunately, they call at Watchet no longer.

In 1861 the harbour was re-designed and rebuilt very much on the same lines as we see it to-day ; one important feature in . the construction of the new harbour was the

PLATE V

GROUP OUTSIDE COTTAGE ON SITE OF PRESENT COUNCIL CHAMBER.   1850-60

PLATE VI

SWAIN STREET, 1860's—LOOKING UP FROM WHAT IS NOW THE WEST SOMERSET HOTEL

complete destruction of yard beach. This was a sandy beach, very popular with visitors and the local children, which extended from a point below Goviers Lane to Splash Point, a portion of which can be seen in the frontispiece to this book. The beach was partly covered by the building of a sea-wall in order to make a harbour boundary, when thousands of tons of rubble were filled in behind to make the present East Wharf. The plans for the new work were prepared by J. Abernethy, M.I.C.E., and the contractor was W. Tredwell. It was at this time that the first industrial dispute occurred in West Somerset. Early in February, 1861, the workmen struck for more wages, and the following account taken from the *West Somerset Free Press* of 9th February, 1861, is worth quoting : ' On Saturday last one of those objectionable " strikes ", alike so injurious to the master and men, took place among the labourers employed in constructing Watchet Harbour. The men, we understand, wanted 3s. 0d. per tide—that is for about five or six hours' work—the contractor appears to be paying 2s. 3d. at present. Some of the men, however, have thought better of the affair, and have returned to their work.' There seems to have been quite a lot of sympathy for the men locally, it being generally agreed that 4¾d. an hour for such dirty work was a gross under-payment.

With the completion of the new harbour in 1861, and the opening of the railway in the following year, a steady expansion of maritime trade was assured. Hundreds of sailing vessels and small steamers entered and left the harbour annually with cargoes of coal, wheat, and other goods, leaving a few days later with timber, flour, paper, and other exports for Liverpool, Ireland, London, and the numerous ports of the Bristol Channel. Together with the considerable exports of iron ore to South Wales it gave the harbour an air of great activity and prosperity.

Roads and Turnpikes

Up to the reign of Queen Anne, in the early years of the eighteenth century, roads as a means of communication had improved little from those of the Middle Ages. The responsibility for keeping roads in repair was still that of the parish, and the farmers of a parish through which a road passed were legally bound to maintain it by six days' unpaid labour annually. One farmer was chosen as surveyor and there was no supervision from outside the parish. The system was anything but satisfactory, the farmers having very little interest in the roads ; work was left undone, or at least partly done, and the general position was that very few well-surfaced roads existed. In fact, the roads of England at that period were vastly inferior to those of the time of the Roman occupation. While it mattered little during the Middle Ages, when horse-riding was general and the pack-horse was commonly used for transporting goods, the increasing development of trade and commerce during the seventeenth century gave a new importance to the highways.

At the beginning of the eighteenth century turnpike companies were formed to take over, repair, and maintain certain sections of the highways. In return for the work they were given legal power to erect toll-gates and levy charges on all traffic using their particular section of road. From 1700 to 1750 over four hundred Road Acts were passed by Parliament, and from 1751 to 1790 a further one thousand six hundred were enacted. In the latter group was an Act continuing a previous Act of 1765, dealing with the roads in this part of West Somerset. The Bill was passed in the 26th year of the reign of George III, 1786, and reads :

A BILL For Continuing the Term, and altering and enlarging the Powers, of an Act, passed in the Fifth Year of His present Majesty's Reign, for repairing and widening several Roads leading from the Port Town and Borough of Minehead, and from Dunster and Watchet, in the County of Somerset.

Whereas an Act was passed in the Fifth Year of this present Majesty's Reign, for repairing, widening, turning, altering, and keeping in Repair, several Roads leading from the Port Town and Borough of Minehead, and from Dunster and Watchet, in the County of Somerset :

And whereas the Term of the said Act is near expiring, and a very considerable Sum of Money hath been borrowed, and is now due and owing, upon the Credit of the said Act ; which Money cannot be repaid, and the said Roads kept in good Repair, unless the said Act be further continued, and some Alterations and Amendments made therein . . .

And whereas it is in and by the said former Act further Enacted, that nothing in that Act contained should extend to impower the said Trustees to erect any Gate or Turnpike between the said Quay and Port Town of Minehead and the Town of Dunster, or between Brendon Hill and the Town of Bampton, on the Watchet Road ; It is hereby further Enacted, That so much of the said recited Act as prohibits the said Trustees from erecting any Gate or Turnpike between Brendon Hill and the Town of Bampton, on the Watchet Road, be, and the same is hereby repealed : Provided, that nothing in this Act contained shall impower the said Commissioners to erect any Gate or Turnpike between a Place called the Five Bells, in the Parish of St. Decuman's, and Raleighs Cross, leading to Bampton.

And it is hereby directed, and the Commissioners are hereby required, from and immediately after the passing of this Act, to apply the Tolls and Duties collected at the said Gate, or at the side Gate, erected or that may hereafter be erected upon the said Road . . . from Watchet to Bampton, in such proportions as they, at their future Meetings, shall direct, but so as at least Half Part of the said Tolls and Duties be applied towards repairing and widening the Road between Watchet and Bampton.

As a result of these Acts three toll-gates were erected within the boundaries of Watchet ; namely, the Five Bells South East Gate, the Five Bells West Gate, and the Watchet West Gate. The first two were situated close to the old Toll House at Five Bells ; the West Gate was probably situated across the road somewhere near the top of what is now Jubilee Terrace. The writer has in his possession two original toll accounts rendered to a Mr. Royall, who

lived at The Green, West Street, at this time. The first
account is for tolls incurred at the West Gate, here is a copy :

		1833	Mr. Royall To T. Burton.		
			For Tolls at Watchet West Gate.		
Oct	8	2 horses & Waggen			1 – 1½
	10	1	Do	J. Court	4½
		Drawing Lime			3 – 0
Nov	22	4 horses & Carege			1 – 6
	23	3	Do	Do	1 – 1½
	25	4	Do	Do	1 – 6
	26	4	Do	Do	1 – 6
	27	4	Do	Do	1 – 6
	29	4	Do	Do	1 – 6
	30	4	Do	Do	1 – 6
Dec	2	4	Do	Do	1 – 6

£0 – 16 – 1½
3 – 6

Settled Thos Burton   12 – 7½
December 9th 1833.

The account for the Five Bells Gate was also made to
Mr. Royall and was due to Joseph Webber. This account
is undated, although I believe we can safely assume that
it is about the same date as the previous account. It covers
a period from 25th May to 17th September, and has many
more entries ; the charges are based on the same rates,
i.e., a four-horse carriage, 1s. 6d. Some new entries on this
account are : a five-horse carriage, 1s. 10½d. ; a one-horse
gig, 4½d. ; one horse, 1½d. ; one donkey cart, 4½d. ; and a
three-horse waggon, 1s. 8d. The total amount for the period
mentioned was £3 7s. 10½d. It was settled on 3rd December
and was signed by Jane Webber.

Most of the turnpikes of the district were owned by
The United Trust of Minehead Roads, and the toll-gates
were let by auction for one or two years at a time. At an
auction of the various gates held at the Luttrell Arms Hotel,
Dunster, on 14th June, 1872, the reserve price for the two
gates at Five Bells, Watchet, was £302. They appear to
have been the most valuable gates in the district ; in contrast,

the Watchet West Gate was only valued at £8 10s. 0d.
The income to the trustees from the toll-gates was considerable, and it was generally considered by the users of
the roads that too little was spent on road repairs. In the
year 1875 the income of The United Minehead Trust was
£1,418, but only a sum of £329 was spent on upkeep, which,
incidentally, was expended over the Williton, Dunster, and
Dulverton districts.

Apparently there was a good deal of agitation at the
time against the tolls, and as a result of the suggestions of
a Select Committee on Turnpikes, which were later embodied
in an Act of Parliament, all the toll-gates administered by
The United Trust of Minehead were abolished. This took
place on 1st November, 1877, when all local roads were
freed, to the great jubilation, as we can imagine, of the
local inhabitants.

The most convenient form of passenger transport was
by stage-coach, and although as yet we have no earlier
records for the district, there is plenty of information about
stage-coaches from the early days of the nineteenth century.
In the year 1829 a mail-coach, supported by public subscription, and called the 'Speculator', was running regularly
between Minehead and Taunton, while by 1840 coaches
were leaving the Plume of Feathers, Minehead, every other
day at 7 a.m. for Bridgwater and Bristol, and at 7.30 a.m.
every day the Taunton Mail left the Wellington Hotel for
Taunton. Information as to whether any of these coaches
came through Watchet is lacking and it seems likely that
intending passengers from Watchet joined the coach at
Williton.

There can be no doubt that Taunton and Bridgwater
were the largest coaching centres of the district, for 'stages'
left both towns daily for London, Bristol, Cheltenham, Bath,
Barnstaple, Plymouth, Falmouth, Bridport, Weymouth,

Sidmouth, and Southampton. Under the prevailing road conditions the times taken for the longer journeys appear to be remarkably good; for example, one of the London coaches, the 'Magnet', left Taunton at '¼ before 6, [a.m.] arriving in London at 9 o'clock in the evening', while the 'Exquisite', which left Taunton at 12.30, arrived at Cheltenham at 9 p.m., and the Falmouth coach, the 'Royal Mail', left Taunton at 3 o'clock, arrived at Falmouth at 11.30 p.m.

A considerable volume of goods was transported by means of the 'Carriers'' carts, and while we have no evidence of any carrier operating directly from Watchet there were no less than three running from Minehead. One left Minehead for Bridgwater and Bristol every Tuesday and Friday, another left for Taunton on the same days and a third ran to Dulverton and Exeter on Tuesdays and Wednesdays. In view of the increasing harbour trade of Watchet at this period it seems strange that no carriers are mentioned, and it may well have been that most of the goods imported through the port were bulky (coal, for instance, was always an important import) ; such goods were probably taken direct to the various towns and villages by the Watchet merchants' waggons, and the lighter goods only collected by the outside carriers.

Social Conditions

The study of the social conditions of a people, by which we mean the portrayal of the daily life of our ancestors and the problems confronting them, is of great importance in general history and of vital concern to our local chronicle. Although we have very few records of the actual social conditions of the people of Watchet up to the fifteenth century, the county records give us some illuminating information from the sixteenth century onwards.

Many readers will probably be surprised to know that price controls were in operation four hundred years ago. In the year 1550, eight years before the accession of Queen Elizabeth I, the Sheriff of the County of Somerset was ordered to proclaim the highest prices at which corn and stock could be sold. The price of best wheat was fixed at 13s. 4d. per quarter and 8s. per quarter for poor quality. Beans were fixed at 5s. to 3s. 8d., while oats sold at 4s. a quarter. The prices for oxen in the same year were from 27s. to 45s. in summer, while the winter prices were from 41s. 4d. to 48s. 4d. Later in the same century, in the years 1585-6, there was a great scarcity of food in the district and a consequent rapid rise in the cost of living; it is recorded that butter rose to 6d. per pound and cheese rose to 3d. The high price and scarcity of corn and bread caused much unrest throughout the countryside, and hungry people raided barns, mills, and granaries, in many cases threshing-out the corn themselves.

The early seventeenth century was a period of great fluctuations in food prices: in the year 1621 wheat was selling at 16s. a bushel, and it is recorded that 'the poor were searching the market for the finest wheat'; yet one year later, in 1622, the price of wheat had risen to 53s. 4d. a bushel and the same people were rioting and attacking farmers on their way to market and taking the corn from them. Some idea of the chaotic state of the corn market can be gathered from the following prices taken over a period of ten years :

```
1621  ...  16s. per bushel.
1622  ...  53s. 4d. ,,
1628  ...  23s.     ,,
1629  ...  32s.     ,,
1630  ...  37s. 11d. ,,
1631  ...  64s.     ,,
```

One of the reasons given at this time for the scarcity of corn was the export of grain to Ireland, and there is a case mentioned in the *Victoria County History of Somerset* of a man loading twenty-four bushels of peas ' secretly into a bark [ship] at Watchett ', covering them with large stones to prevent discovery of his cargo, and then sailing under cover of darkness.

Wages were also controlled in the seventeenth century, and we read that in the year 1685 the Somerset County Magistrates fixed the following wages :

Men Servants	£4 : 10 : 0	per annum.
Women Servants	£2 : 10 : 0	,, ,,
Mowers (finding themselves)*	1s. 2d.	per day.
,, (at meat and drink)†	7d.	,, ,,
Haymakers (finding themselves)	7d.	,, ,,
,, (at meat and drink)	4d.	,, ,,
Reapers (finding themselves)	1s. 2d.	,, ,,
,, (at meat and drink)	8d.	,, ,,
Masons, Carpenters, Tilers and Thatchers from		
15th March to 15th September	1s. 2d.	,, ,,
from 15th September to 15th March ...	1s. 0d.	,, ,,

[These rates were for ' finding themselves '.]
[The rates for piece work varied according to the nature of the crop, as the following list shows :]

Mowing one acre of Grass	1s. 2d.
Making one acre of Hay	1s. 6d.
Mowing one acre of Barley	1s. 1d.
Reaping and binding one acre of Wheat ...	3s. 0d.
Cutting and binding one acre of Beans ...	2s. 0d.
Drawing one acre of Hemp	4s. 6d.

* Providing their own food.
† Food provided by employer.

A century later wages were about the same, the average wage for agricultural workers in the year 1771 was one shilling per day all the year round, with an allowance of beer or cider and extra food at haymaking and harvest.

Food prices at Taunton recorded in the year 1794 were, for the best beef, veal, and mutton, 4d. per pound in winter, 3½d. per pound in summer. Turkeys were sold for three shillings and sixpence each, geese three shillings each, while ducks and fowls were half-a-crown and two shillings a pair respectively. A reference to conditions in Watchet was made at this time by Arthur Young, a prominent agricultural writer of the period. He wrote: 'In 1795 Welsh coal was selling at Watchet at 8d. per bushel. The poor however burned wood, or tanners old bark, made into square pieces and called tan turfs, as well as turfs cut from the Quantocks.'

While such food prices appear to us absurdly low they must be considered in relation to the wages prevailing. A labourer earning six shillings for his week's work, out of which he had to feed, clothe, and house his family, was, obviously, quite unable to buy a turkey at three shillings and sixpence. In fact, the foregoing quotations show that living conditions of the ordinary worker were extremely hard a century and a half ago. Poverty in the countryside was general, an instance of which is given in the findings of an enquiry made by Sir Frederick Eden into the circumstances of several families living in the Stogursey area at the end of the eighteenth century. He found that the incomes of these families were well below the amount required to feed, clothe, and house them. He wrote, 'Their clothing was of the poorest character, they can spare little and waste their time in patching rags.'

One of the greatest causes of distress at this time was the implementing of the Enclosure Acts. These Acts deprived labourers of fuel from the wastes and commons, reduced the number of small-holders, and prevented cottagers from running their pigs, geese, and other animals on the commons and wastes. The economic effect of this was that large numbers of countrymen, who had formerly been self-supporting (doing occasional and seasonal work in addition to working their small-holdings), were turned into labourers almost overnight.

Naturally much bitterness and hostility were shown towards the landowners and their friends by the small-holders and the rural population. It is nicely exemplified by the following piece of doggerel, popular during the period :

' The law locks up the man or woman
Who steals the goose from off the common ;
But leaves the greater villain loose
Who steals the common from the goose.'

Demonstrations, and serious riots, were frequent in many parts of the country from the middle of the eighteenth century until the early part of the nineteenth century, but we have no records of any enclosure troubles from Watchet. The probable reason was that Watchet's importance was based on the import and export of goods and raw materials through the port. With agriculture taking a place of secondary importance, it seems likely that the common lands had gradually been enclosed over a long period without much serious opposition from the townsfolk.

The period was also one of great political and economic change. The American War of Independence, in which the American colonies broke away from England, was followed by the French Revolution in 1789-95. This last event had a profound effect on radical and progressive thought in this country. We can well imagine discussions taking place over a pot of ale in one of Watchet's inns as news of the great happenings was received.

An instance of the political repercussions in West Somerset is that given in the accounts of the lives of Coleridge and Wordsworth. In the year 1796 Coleridge came to live at Nether Stowey ; he was followed a year later by Words-worth and his sister Dorothy, who rented Alfoxton House, near Holford. Both Coleridge and Wordsworth, like many progressive intellectuals of their time, were sympathetic to the ideals of the French Revolution. Coleridge's political opinions were particularly suspect to the government of the day, so much so that a spy was sent down from London to watch him and the many literary friends who came to visit him. Government circles and their supporters in the country were extremely frightened by, and often quite hysterical over, the English sympathizers; when Wordsworth's lease of Alfoxton expired in 1798 a renewal was refused, presumably on the grounds that he was regarded as a potential traitor. After leaving Holford the Wordsworths travelled in Germany for some months, and on their return to England settled at Grasmere in the Lake District. The story is told that when they were living in West Somerset they planned a walking-tour over the Quantocks to Watchet, Minehead, Porlock, and Lynmouth with Coleridge. To defray the expenses of the holiday they decided to write poetry, and as they approached Watchet the idea of a sea-poem took shape which eventually matured as Coleridge's poem *The Ancient Mariner*.

Generally there was much discontent among the mass of the people, and the industrial revolution was having a profound effect on rural industries. Goods were being manufactured in the new factories much quicker and cheaper than was possible by hand; in consequence the village weaver, for instance, could not compete with the cloth being manufactured by the power-looms. The same applied to most of the other industries and crafts, and in districts which were becoming rapidly industrialized village craftsmen were driven by economic circumstances into the mills; in rural areas the position of local craftsmen was even worse, and the combined effect of enclosures and industrial revolution was widespread poverty and distress.

Records of the County Assizes clearly reflect the fear in which landless labourers were held by the ruling class

of the time.   Here are a few of the savage sentences meted
out to some of the unfortunate people of West Somerset
in the year 1784.   A man was hanged at Taunton for stealing
a watch, while another, also at Taunton, was transported
for seven years for stealing a shirt.   In 1801 nine men were
hanged on the stone gallows at Wellington for stealing bread.
Punishments for ' minor ' offences were public whippings,
standing in the pillory, and branding with hot irons on the
forehead and hand.

That similar conditions prevailed in and around Watchet
well into the nineteenth century is shown by two interesting
documents published locally.   The first was compiled in
1834 and was signed by Robert Leigh and Thomas Warden
of Bardon.   The preamble to this document is as follows :

> RULES of the Saint Decuman's, Bicknoller, Crowcombe,
> East Quantoxhead, Monksilver, Nettlecombe, Old Cleeve,
> Samford Brett, Stogumber, and West Quantoxhead Association
> for the Protection of Property from Plunder.

> The object of this Association being the detecting, appre-
> hending, and prosecuting of all persons, who shall commit,
> or who shall aid in, abet, or be accessory to any of the offences
> hereafter specified, against or upon the Persons or Property
> of any Subscriber, there shall and may *for the more speedy and
> effectual discovery of any such offender or offenders*, be paid
> from the Funds of this Association, to any Person or Persons
> upon whose Information and Evidence, any such Offender or
> Offenders, or any or either of his, her, or their Aiders, Abbettors,
> or Accessories, shall be convicted, of the Offences aforesaid
> respectively, the following Rewards.

> (i)   Wilfully and maliciously burning or setting fire to any
>   House, Barn, Hovel, Cock, Mow, or Stack of Corn,
>   Straw, Hay or Wood.   £10 – 10 – 0.
> (ii) Sending any Letter without Name subscribed thereto,
>   or signed with a fictitious Name, threatening to burn
>   any House etc.   £10 – 10 – 0.
> (iii) Highway-Robbery, Burglary, House-breaking, stealing,
>   killing, maiming, or maliciously wounding any Horse,
>   Mare, Gelding, Sheep, Pig or Cattle.   £5 – 0 – 0.
> (iv) Stealing any kind of Corn or Grain, after it has been
>   harvested, or in sacks.   £5 – 0 – 0.
> (v)   Stealing any kind of Corn or Grain before harvested.
>   Stealing or killing, Turkies, Geese, Fowls, Ducks, or
>   Eggs.   Stealing in any Garden or Orchard, any other

Property than Apples. Stealing any Implement of
Husbandry, Measures, or Working Tools, or any sort
of Hay, Straw or Reed.   £1 – 10 – 0.
(*vi*)   Stealing any Turnips, Potatoes, Cabbage, Carrots, Peas
or Beans, or any Gates, Hurdles, Bars, Shuts, Hooks
or Eyes of Gates, Faggot Wood etc.   10 – 6.
(*vii*) Stealing Apples.   10 – 6.
(*viii*) Stealing or cutting Bow Sticks, Saplings etc.
£1 – 1 – 0.
(*ix*)   Breaking, cutting, and tearing Hedges.   5 – 0.
(*x*)   Stealing, or receiving Cloth, stealing Cloth in Racks.
£5 – 5 – 0.

Signed Robert Leigh, Thomas Warden.
Secretaries and Treasurers, Bardon.

Such substantial rewards being offered by the landowners, farmers, and merchants, to obtain convictions
plainly points to a general unrest in the locality ; while
the mention in rule (*x*) of stealing ' Cloth in Racks ' is
additional proof that cloth was still being manufactured
in the locality.

Four years later the following letter was addressed :

*To the Inhabitants and Rate-Payers of the Parish of St.
Decuman's.*
Sirs,
We, the undersigned, being the Guardians of the Poor
of the said Parish, beg respectfully to call your attention to
the very advanced price of all the Necessaries of Life, and to
the present inequality and in many cases inadequacy of Wages
paid to Labourers in this Parish.
By the operation of the Poor Law Amendment Act No
Relief can be granted to an able-bodied-Pauper, for and on
account of himself or Family out of the Union Workhouse,
except in case of Sickness or Accident.
This regulation, although proper on principle, causes at
this time with the present rate of wages, some individual cases
of suffering, which we are anxious to remove.
Will you do us the favour to meet us at the Market-House
in Watchet, on Friday next the 21st day of December, at the
hour of 4 in the afternoon precisely, to consider of the best
means of promoting so desirable an object,

We are, Sirs,

Your obedient Servants,

John. Pulman.
Wm. James.

Doniford, Dec 15th, 1838.

PLATE VII

THE RAILWAY STATION IN THE 1860's, SHOWING ENGINE SHED AND WATER TANK

PLATE VIII

CELEBRATING THE RE-OPENING OF THE WEST SOMERSET MINERAL RAILWAY,
4th JULY, 1907

CHAPTER FIVE

WATCHET IN THE NINETEENTH CENTURY

Some People and their Occupations

DURING the nineteenth century several minor industries make their appearance in Watchet. In a letter written in 1843 by the townspeople to the Earl of Litchfield, then Postmaster-General, mention is made not only of woollen manufacture but also of the export of leather and of the import of hides. These facts suggest that in addition to the making of yarn and the weaving of cloth there may also have been a tanyard in the town.

The reason prompting the sending of the letter was to complain that the town had no post office; apparently Watchet seems to have been worse off than it was about two centuries earlier when Thomas Witherstone, His Majesty's Postmaster to Charles I, organized a system of mail routes and post towns throughout the country. Under this scheme Watchet was one of twenty-four post towns in Somerset, other West Somerset towns in the list being Minehead and Dunster. These places were certainly well favoured, for the whole of the coastal area between Bridgwater and Bristol was unprovided for, and letters had to be taken to Bristol or Wells as the nearest post towns. The charge for a letter of a single sheet was 3d.; if under eighty miles 2d.; and for letters of greater bulk 8d. per ounce.

The letter which the people of Watchet sent to the Earl of Litchfield is given in full below, because it presents an interesting picture of the trade and commerce of the town just over a century ago :

> *To the Right Honorable the Earl of Litchfield, Post Master General.*
>
> My Lord,
>
> We the undersigned Inhabitants and Traders of the Sea Port Town of Watchet, in the County of Somersetshire, and its neighbourhood, feeling the very great inconvenience and additional expense of having no Post Office beg to represent to your Lordship our grievance in this respect, and to solicit the establishment of one forthwith, as the increasing trade and commerce of the place calls for such a step.
>
> There are nine Vessels belonging to the Port trading to Bristol, Liverpool, Ireland and the different Ports of Wales. The export of Corn, Timber, Flour, Malt, Leather etc, and the import of Coal, Hides and Merchandize is very considerable. The Port is frequently visited by Vessels of large burthen. There are also connected with the place extensive Paper and Corn Mills, Woollen Manufactory etc. The population of the Town is nearly a thousand. The present Post Office is situated at Williton, two miles distant, which is extremely inconvenient.
>
> We therefore respectfully solicit your Lordships attention to the Object of our Petition.

This being only a copy of the letter sent no names were appended, which is unfortunate as a list of the petitioners would have been of great interest. We can, however, assume that most of the people named in the list of principal inhabitants of 1840 (page 107) would have been signatories.

The earliest directory list of the principal inhabitants of Watchet appeared in *The Universal British Directory of Trade, Commerce, and Manufacture*, published in 1794. This is as follows :

Besley, Nathaniel.	Linen-draper.
Burton, Thomas.	Cordwainer.
Bryant, Ann.	Miller.
Gimblett, Margaret.	Coal-merchant.
Jenkins, John.	,,
Michell, Joan and Margaret.	Clothiers.
Priest, Eleanor.	Linen-draper.
Pulman, William.	Coal-merchant.
Potter, William.	Inn-keeper. (The Bell.)
Quick, William.	Tide-waiter.
Sibley, John.	Edge-tool maker.
Trott, William.	Landwaiter of Customs.

Tanner, Nicholas.	Maltster.
Welch, Thomas.	Coal-merchant.
Wheddon, Thomas.	,,
Winter, John.	,,
Wills, Matthew.	Tanner.
Wood, William.	Paper-maker.

It is noticeable that there are no gentry, lawyers, clergy, or physicians mentioned, although Minehead, Taunton, and other towns in the neighbourhood seem to have been well provided with such gentlemen at this time.

A similar list was again published in the year 1840, by the proprietors of the *Somerset County Gazette*, Taunton, in their General Directory for the County of Somerset. It shows a considerable increase in the number and variety of business interests, and we can assume that there had been a steady expansion of the town's commerce in the period covered.

Francis, Jenkins.	Custom Officer.
Peter, Boswell.	Water Bailiff.
Flee, Arthur.	Baker.
Whitehorn, Thomas.	Bookseller and Printer.
Burton, Richard.	Boot and Shoemaker.
Burton, Thomas.	Do.
Perry, John.	Do.
Williams, George.	Do.
Ridler, Thomas.	Butcher.
Jones, James.	Carpenter.
Geen, George.	China and Glass-dealer.
Date, John.	Coal-merchant.
Gimblett, John.	Do.
Gimblett, William.	Do.
Govier, John.	Do.
Hole, George.	Do.
Stoate, Thomas.	Do. and Corn-dealer.
Cavill, George.	Draper.
Date, James.	Draper and Grocer.
Williams & Co.	Drapers.
Norman, William.	General Shopkeeper.
Prees, Thomas.	Do.
Cadell, Thomas.	Gentleman.
Govett, Mr.	Land Surveyor.
Pasmore, Jane.	Lodging Housekeeper.
Hole, H. G.	Malster and Merchant.

Hole, W. G.	Merchant.
Moore, Robert.	Do.
Wheddon, Ann.	Do.
Potter, Robert.	Miller.
Organ, Luke.	Mill-Puff Manufacturer.
Poole, Rev. Robert.	Vicar of St. Decuman's.
Sutton, Rev. S.	Baptist Minister.
Wansbrough, Peach & Date.	Paper-makers.
Siderfin, Robert.	Saddler & Harness-maker.
Browning, John.	Smith.
Davis, William.	Do.
Sully, Samuel.	Do.
Rale, Henry.	Surgeon.
Chidgey, Henry.	Tailor.
Chitty, Henry.	Do.
Cox, Henry.	Do.
Royall, George.	Timber Merchant.
Young, Thomas.	Do.
Hurley, James.	Wheelwright.
Pulman, Thomas.	Woollen-manufacturer.

An analysis of these lists shows some interesting features; in the first, for instance, we see that out of the fifteen business houses mentioned four are owned by women, one of whom is the miller and another a coal-merchant. In the second list, published forty-six years later, only two women appear, Ann Wheddon, a merchant, and Jane Pasmore, a lodging-house keeper. Despite the fact that women appear to have dropped some of their business interests in the intervening years (these are the only two in a list of forty), they were evidently capable at managing the inns, for in another list of 1840 we see that three of the six inns were held by women.

This list is taken from a *General Directory for the County of Somerset*, published by Wm. Bragg, 1840, and gives the following Watchet inns :

Anchor.	Gowin Baker.
Bell.	Mrs. Nicholas.
Greyhound.	Sarah H. Watts.
New London.	T. Young.
Sailors Delight.	Ann Bryce.
Star.	Wm. Watts.

The second list also gives Watchet two ministers of religion, a surgeon, and one member of the ' gentry or private families ' as they were listed. The town, however, was still unable to boast of a member of the legal profession.

There were several other inns in Watchet in former days, and some still existed when the tithe map was revised in 1841. The Greyhound Inn stood on the site of Hooper's butcher's shop ; when this shop was being rebuilt and altered a few years ago a large fireplace was found and a quantity of churchwarden clay pipes. Two doors away fiom the Greyhound, towards the harbour, was the George Inn. The Ship Inn was situated in Market Street, on the site of Melbourne House. Seventeenth-century records mention the Sailors' Delight and the Blew Anchor–the latter might have been on the site of the present Anchor Hotel. The writer has not, however, been able to trace the site of the Sailors' Delight, despite the fact that according to the above-mentioned list it was still occupied in 1840.

The Poor Law

Watchet appears to lack any early records of poor-law administration. We have, however, particulars taken from neighbouring churchwardens' account books, which are most informative, and give us an idea of conditions that must also have existed at Watchet in the eighteenth century. In a paper read at Old Cleeve by the late Mr. Clement Kille, of Minehead, many examples of accounts were given relating to the management of the Old Cleeve Workhouse. In the year 1731, for example, ' tobacco for ye poor ' was ninepence a pound, twenty-one pounds of mutton five shillings, twenty-two pounds of cheese three shillings and twopence halfpenny, forty-six pounds of beef seven shillings and twopence halfpenny. Butter was fourpence halfpenny a pound, and potatoes eightpence a peck. Pork appeared to be the most expensive meat ; half of a pig, weighing one hundred and eighty-three pounds, cost one pound, ten shillings and sixpence. His paper also contained the following account of the funeral expenses of a workhouse inmate as follows :

'July 1731. Making ye grave and tolling ye bell for Gabrell Baker 1s.
Gabrell Baker's coffin 7s.
For bear [beer] for them that helpt Gabrell Baker to church 3s.
For carrying ye bear [bier] up to Road-water for ye same Baker 1s.
For straching him forth 6d.
Affidavit for ye same Baker 1s.'

Following the introduction of the modern poor-law system in 1834 we have more information concerning Watchet. Out-Relief was administered in St. Decuman's parish by the Williton Board of Guardians. One of their rules was : ' that on all applications for relief, inquiries shall be made if the person applying have not relatives of their own who are in a situation to assist them and bound by law to do so, and if they have, such relatives shall be requested to come forward for that purpose.' The scale of out-relief adopted by the Board in 1836 was : ' To an aged person of seventy years and upwards incapable of work, but still moving about, one shilling and sixpence and one loaf. To an aged person, wholly incapable of doing anything, two shillings and a loaf. To a married couple, wholly incapable of work, three shillings and sixpence and two loaves. To an able-bodied labourer, having four children under ten years of age, and whose wife is incapable of work, one loaf. To a single person, incapacitated from labour by sickness, one shilling and sixpence and one loaf. To an orphan child, under ten years of age, one shilling and one loaf. To an orphan child, above ten years of age, and unable to maintain itself, sixpence and one loaf.'

At a meeting of the Guardians in September, 1836, concern was expressed at the 'numerous and increasing applications for relief to the Board by mothers of illegitimate children', in fact, it was stated that 'at present there are eighty-five mothers of illegitimate children and ninety-two such children receiving relief, and that an increased number is likely to be placed on the list.' As a result it was agreed that steps should be taken to procure a temporary work-house (this was, of course, before the erection of the work-house at Williton), and accordingly a meeting of the Guardians was held at St. Decuman's; they reported that the St. Decuman's Poor-house was capable of affording good accommodation for thirty-two beds and might be fitted up ready for reception of such paupers at an expense not exceeding £10. It was also recommended that the overseers of the parish of St. Decuman's should be paid £15 a year, and the churchwardens £5 a year as compensation and rent for the Poor-house. A month later at the Board's meeting it was stated that the churchwardens of St. Decuman's had refused to let the Poor-house on these terms.

The site of the Poor-house was directly opposite the cottages at St. Decuman's; it was a long building and was built on land that is now part of the churchyard. In the tithe map prepared in 1838, and revised in 1841, the building is marked number 1154, but in the Tithe Apportionment List it is described as 'The Fair House (Churchwardens) Occupiers the poor' and is marked 'void'.

Despite the fact that distress was prevalent at this time, and that living conditions of the workers and their families must have been extremely difficult, no effort seems to have been spared to celebrate any important event in a festive and picturesque way, as is shown by a poster issued in Watchet to commemorate the coronation of Queen Victoria :

The
CORONATION
of
Her Most Gracious Majesty
QUEEN VICTORIA,
on Thursday, June 28th, 1838.
This Event Will be Commemorated
by
A PUBLIC TEA.
With Salt Herrings,
To be held on the Green in front of
Mr. Royall's House, at Watchet.
As many of the neighbourhood may wish to attend who
are not Subscribers, Tickets, One Shilling each, may be
had at Mr. James Dait's, or at Mr. T. Whitehorne's.
No admittance without Tickets.
BEEF AND ALE
Will be provided for those who can pay for it.
The Stringston Band will attend.
GOD SAVE THE QUEEN

The programme for the day makes very interesting
reading, especially the order of the procession. This was
headed by ' Eight rows of girls, four abreast, with a man on
each side to keep them in order ', then followed boys, women,
and men, then more girls, etc.; between each section boys
carried banners on which such slogans as ' God Bless Our
Queen ', ' God Bless The Plough ', etc., were inscribed.
The procession, headed by the band, moved off to a given
point where the band stopped, the procession then formed
around it, a verse of ' God Save the Queen ' was then sung,
followed by cheering ; this was repeated until The Cross
was reached, where apparently several verses of the National
Anthem were sung, accompanied with extra cheers. The
procession then marched back to Mr. Royall's house at the

Green, where we hope they did justice to the ' Salt Herrings, Beef and Ale '.

Up to the beginning of the nineteenth century the economic position of Watchet seems to have altered very little over the centuries. Trade, as in past centuries, was still centred in and around the harbour, and many families must have depended directly for their livelihood on the ships which the husbands and sons manned. Other families had probably been shipwrights and shipbuilders for generations. Carpenters, blacksmiths, and masons would also have shared in the work connected with the harbour. An interesting example of a family's continual connexion with a particular craft over the centuries is that of the Chidgey family of Watchet, members of which have been masons and builders until quite recently. The Chidgeys were masons as far back as 1715, when it is on record that ' Madam Luttrell ', in an agreement dated 10th May of that year, employed ' Thomas Chidgey, a mason of Watchett ', to repair the damage caused by rough weather to the harbour at Minehead. In addition to those dependent on the harbour there were those employed in agriculture and the smaller industries.

The population of Watchet is not easy to assess for the period prior to the formation of the Urban District Council in 1902. Figures available are those for the ecclesiastical parish of St. Decuman's, which comprised Watchet, Williton, Doniford, and Stream. The figure given in the official census of 1801 for the parish is 1,602. It is probably safe to assume that the population of Watchet would have been about half this number.

Another, and quite different, assessment of the population of Watchet in the early part of the nineteenth century is given in C. & J. Greenwood's book *Somerset*, published in 1822 ; they state that the parish of St. Decuman's includes the port of Watchet which contains three hundred and sixty inhabited houses, occupied by three hundred and eighty-five families, one hundred and seventy-seven of whom are employed in agriculture, one hundred and ninety in trade, manufacture or handicraft and eighteen not included in either class.

The record, if accurate, gives a considerable increase in the population of the town over a period of twenty years ; for if we reckon the average family to be four persons, a conservative estimate for those days, we should have a population in Watchet of 1,540. The high proportion of families employed in agriculture, one hundred and seventy-seven, inclines the writer to doubt the accuracy of the figures, for at the most there would not have been more than five or six farms in the town at this period, and one hundred and seventy-seven families cannot have been dependent on them. The probable explanation is that the Greenwoods' figures were for the whole of St. Decuman's parish, which would thus explain the high proportion of persons engaged in agriculture. A more acceptable figure is given in the Somerset section of Pigott's Directory, for 1830, where it is stated that the inhabitants of St. Decuman's parish number 1,865, of which about 600 belong to Watchet.

Nonconformity

Towards the end of the eighteenth century the Nonconformist movement began to take root in the West Country, where ever since it has had quite a strong following. In W. Symon's book *Early Methodism in West Somerset*, it is stated that there were four converts in the Minehead and Watchet district as early as 1791. At the outset there appeared to have been a great deal of persecution and coercion by the employers and landowners against the adherents of Nonconformity, but despite this the new movement advanced. Lady Huntingdon's evangelists were

PLATE IX

THE HARBOUR BEFORE THE ESPLANADE WAS RAILED.

PLATE X

SAILING SHIPS IN THE 19TH CENTURY

apparently the local pioneers of Methodism and, at Watchet, from a handful of converts there quickly grew the largest group in the district. At a quarterly meeting held in Watchet on 23rd April, 1823, it was resolved : ' That it is the opinion of this meeting that a Chapel is necessary in Watchet and that one be built on the land bought of Mr. Williams immediately.'

Among ardent supporters of Lady Huntingdon's preachers was a Mr. Palmer, who purchased two cottages (on the site of the present Baptist Chapel). These he converted into a ' Meeting Place ' (as chapels were generally termed). The ' Meeting Place ' was used until 1824, when the present Baptist Chapel was erected on the same site, most of the people using the building having transferred their allegiance to the Baptist faith. As the original deed for the premises stipulated that under certain circumstances this chapel should pass to the Methodists, a discussion took place as to whether a legal claim should be made for the new building ; it was, however, eventually decided to proceed with the building of a second chapel rather than become involved in litigation. The new Methodist Chapel, later to become the Salvation Army Hall (now the Home Guard Club), was opened on 1st August, 1825.

An interesting connexion with the paper industry may be noted with the publication, by Thomas Hawkes in the year 1831, of a collection of tunes for the Methodist hymn-book. This was printed at Watchet on paper specially made for the purpose at the Watchet paper-mill. Several members of the Wood family, the earliest known paper-makers, were strong supporters of Methodism, as also were the later owners of the mills, Messrs. Wansbrough, Peach, and Date. Another local family closely connected with the Methodist Chapel was the Stoate family; their name occurs in the records of the movement from the earliest days. The present chapel in Station Road was opened in 1871.

The Baptist denomination have without interruption continued to use the chapel built by Lady Huntingdon's followers in 1824, though it appears that, should circumstances arise whereby they ceased to exist as a separate denomination, the chapel reverts to the Wesleyan Methodists according to the original agreement still held by the trustees of the Baptist Chapel.

The Bible Christians, or United Methodists, were late to establish themselves at Watchet, and when they did so it was largely due to the efforts of one lady, a Miss Rich, who came from Spaxton to live in the town. In the year 1859 she formed a society of twenty members, and on 3rd October of that year the foundation stone of the Temple Chapel was laid by Mr. Isaac Wood. As a result of a dispute over the terms of the trust deed the chapel then closed for a period, but reopened in 1866, and a resident preacher was appointed. The Rev. R. Kelly, known in the locality as 'Happy Dick', was appointed to the chapel in 1868; he appears to have been a great revivalist and more than doubled the chapel membership in a very short time. Although the movement was never very strong in Watchet, it had a number of faithful followers among the workers and businessmen of the town.

The field to the south of this chapel, then known as Hooper's field, was the venue of the first open-air meeting held by the Salvation Army in Watchet. From this meeting, held in 1882, several local enthusiasts joined the new denomination, continuing with meetings in their homes as well as open-air meetings in various parts of the town. Eventually the old Methodist chapel was taken over as their headquarters and the first officers were appointed to Watchet on 31st July, 1884. It is interesting to note that the names of the officers were Captain Castle and Lieutenant Hall, which explains why, from that date until quite recently, the building was always known in Watchet as the Castle Hall.

The Bethel Flag

A rather diverting incident occurred in 1823, when a dispute arose between the local sailors and the customs officers of Watchet and Minehead. A religious organization known as the Brotherhood of the Sea was formed locally, and one of their number, a Captain Wilkins, of Watchet, designed a flag, to be used as a signal for divine service. During May and June, 1823, services were held at Minehead on board the ship, *Fair Trader*, when the flag of the brotherhood—which bore the word ' Bethel ' in large letters on a blue ground, with a yellow star above and a dove with an olive branch beneath—was run up to the masthead. The local customs officers were outraged, informing the sailors concerned that they were unauthorized to use the flag and that they were liable to a fine of £500.

The sailors immediately wrote to the president of the British and Foreign Seamen's Friendly Society, in London, in which the above society had been merged, and the president, Lord Gambier, replied that should there be any further interference he would approach the government for redress. The Watchet branch of the society decided to make a test-case and, holding a meeting on Captain William Gimblett's sloop, *The Sociable Friend*, in Watchet harbour, hoisted the Bethel flag to the masthead. Immediately the customs officers came on the scene and insisted that the flag be hauled down. The upshot of the incident was that Lord Gambier approached the Commissioners of the Customs and an order was sent to the local officers directing them to refrain from such interference in the future.

An illuminating footnote to the above story is the attitude of the local landowners to unorthodox religions. According to reports it seems that both Lord King of Porlock, and Lord Egremont of Watchet, ' grants free permission to every man that he may worship God according to the dictates of his own conscience ', but at Minehead ' it is almost certain ruin that any family shall presume to embrace an opinion, or seek for a chapel at all diverse to the views of the landholder.'

Education

There is little evidence of much in the way of educational facilities at Watchet before the latter half of the nineteenth century. No doubt small ' dame's schools ' existed earlier at which some sort of learning was imparted to local youth, but the first school of which we have any certain information was that established by Mr. R. Bond, then a leader in the first Methodist class at Watchet, about 1826. The school, probably one of the larger houses, was situated in Swain Street, and catered for ' boarders ' as well as day pupils. Mr. Bond eventually became a Methodist minister. About the same time, or a little later, a ' young ladies' academy ' was opened, the principal of which was Mrs. Whitehorn. She was, no doubt, the wife of Watchet's first printer, Mr. T. Whitehorn. Some years later a Mr. Edmund Chitty was running a school for boys here, and during the eighteen-fifties a school for girls was established in Sea View Terrace by a Mrs. Westcombe.

The first day schools appear to have been opened during the eighteen-seventies, the Council School in the rooms below the Methodist Church in Station Road; the school continued there until the new school, now the County School, was opened in 1909. The Church of England School was built and opened during the years 1873–4.

The Watchet Hobblers and Friendly Societies

One of the oldest and best-known associations in Watchet is that of the ' Hobblers', and while the date of its founding is unknown it is probable that it has been in existence for several centuries. The origin of the name is unknown, but one likely explanation is that it may be a corruption of the term ' hovellers', used by the old Kentish and Sussex boatmen. However that may be, the functions of both hobblers and hovellers were the same, to meet, guide, and help ships into port. There seem to have been several rival groups at Watchet prior to 1863, but in that year a United Sailors' Society was formed and definite rules established. At a meeting held on 18th March at the London Inn, the shareholders of the hobble boats agreed ' that the three boats be put into a club to be called the " United Sailors' Society ", for the mutual benefit of those who now hold a share or shares in the boats.'

Earnings were shared on an agreed basis, the boat at each hobble taking a man's share, while a member of the society was appointed to care for the boats for the sum of twelve shillings a year. Contributions were paid by members for sick benefits, and a general levy of sixpence was made on all on the death of a member, but with the advent of registered friendly societies this part of the society's work was abandoned. An annual dinner was also held at the London Inn on Whit-Monday. Although its activities are now greatly reduced, the Association still functions.

Friendly Societies

Like most towns and villages of the West Country Watchet had its share of friendly, or mutual assistance, societies. The earliest that the writer has been able to trace appears to be the Re-Union Club, which was established at Watchet in 1849. The rules of the club, which were printed

by Samuel Cox in 1859, give many interesting details of
the functions undertaken by the club. Membership was
limited to men between the ages of sixteen and forty years
of age, who on joining were required to pay an admission
fee of three shillings and sixpence, and thereafter a contri-
bution of one shilling and threepence monthly ; an additional
sixpence was levied on all members on the death of a member,
or of a member's wife. Sick benefit was paid out at the rate
of nine shillings a·week for twelve months, after which the
sum was reduced to two shillings and sixpence a week.
Funeral expenses were paid up to seven pounds for a member,
and up to four pounds for a member's wife. There were
numerous rules, the breaking of any one of which made the
member liable to a fine. The following is an example :
' . . . any member who shall offer to lay a wager, or play
at any sort of game, or who shall curse or swear, or use any
obscene or provoking language or come into the club-room
in a state of intoxication, or shall quarrel or strike another
member, or refuse to be silent and sit down at the desire
of the secretary or either of the stewards during meeting
hours . . . '. A breach of any part of the above rule made
the member liable to a fine of one shilling.

The latter half of the nineteenth century brought a
great deal of ' Club ' and ' Society ' activity, all of which
was well reported in the *West Somerset Free Press*. On the
9th of January, 1866, we read that ' the Loyal St. Decuman's
Lodge of Foresters with visiting brethren of Court Dunster
Castle and visiting Oddfellows paraded the streets of Williton.
The procession included the Chief Ranger, two mounted
Foresters, the band of the 11th Somerset Rifle Volunteers
(Stowey), Oddfellows, car containing Robin Hood and
Maid Marion, flag, Foresters, a floral device, band of
Somerset Rifle Volunteers (Minehead), mounted Foresters,
and Foresters on foot.'

On the 26th May of the same year the Watchet United
Sailors Benefit Society held their annual parade, followed
by a dinner at their headquarters at the London Inn,
seventy-six members attended. This society was founded
in 1864, for we read that the ninth annual celebrations were
held the 25th of May, 1872, when the members, wearing
rosettes and headed by the band of the 9th Somerset
Volunteers, walked to church and afterwards returned to
their headquarters for dinner. The Anchor Hotel was the
headquarters of the Independent Friendly Society, who held
their club-walk in June. An account in the *West Somerset
Free Press*, June, 1873, states that both societies paraded,
there being eighty and fifty-three members in the procession
respectively.

There was great enthusiasm at this time among the
adherents of various temperance organizations. In 1872,
one of these, the Good Templars, purchased the Old Wesleyan
Chapel (now the Home Guard Club) for the use of their
order and as a public lecture room. The society included a
juvenile section which was called the Cold Water Templars.
On the 21st of June, 1873, we have an account of a great
temperance rally which took place on the Pleasure Ground.
Excursion trains, from Taunton and the Mineral Railway,
brought hundreds of people into Watchet, while a steamer
from Cardiff brought another hundred, including the Bute
Temperance Band. The procession, marshalled on the
Esplanade, included the Monksilver Band, visiting members
of the Independent Order of Good Templars, Watchet New
Lifeboat Lodge of Good Templars, the Henry Gale Lodge,
Watchet Teetotal Society, the Bute Band, Juvenile Templars,
Watchet Band of Hope, and the Williton Band of Hope.
The procession totalled about six hundred in all.

The temperance movement remained very much alive
until the end of the century. In March, 1890, a jubilee of

the Watchet Teetotal Society was commemorated by meetings and a tea. At one of these meetings it was stated that the first meeting of the society was held on the 13th of February, 1840, in the Market House room, and that within three and a half years of that date the membership of the society had grown to 245 members. It is interesting to note that as late as 1893 the Market House was used for similar meetings, for in March of that year Captain A. F. Luttrell, of East Quantoxhead, and Mr. R. J. Thorne, of Watchet, were initiated honorary members of the ' Morning Star ' Tent of the Independent Order of the Rechabites.

Many institutions, such as these friendly societies, have now become social activities of a past era, their origins, deeply bound up with the church festivals and guilds of the Middle Ages, being now forgotten. Several club-walks have continued in the surrounding district until recent years, but the end of the nineteenth century also saw the end in Watchet of associations which had probably been in existence for many centuries.

St. Decuman's Fair (Watchet Fair)

Occasional references occur in early records relating to Watchet of a fair, or market, which was apparently in existence as early as the thirteenth century. According to a note in the Close Rolls of Henry III, an attempt was made to establish a market at Watchet, but his government caused it to be suppressed without delay, on the grounds that it might be injurious to a market which had just been established at Dunster, by the lord of that place, Reynold de Mohun, who was at that time a ward of the Crown. It seems doubtful, however, whether this attempt succeeded because in 1243, while King Henry was still on the throne, we find in ' Somerset Pleas ' of that period (Somerset Record Society, Vol. II) that the bailiffs of the city of Exeter met in that year to consider why Nicholas de Evesham took

PLATE XI

SWAIN STREET IN THE EARLY 1900s.

PLATE XII

WATCHET HARBOUR WRECKED BY A GALE IN 1901

tolls from some of the lawful men of Exeter who came to the fair at St. Decuman's. In 1407 there is further evidence of such an institution, for in that year one of the Sheriff's summoners, John Dolle, served a writ on a local man ' in open market at Watchet'.

There is no doubt that for centuries an annual fair was held at Watchet, and it is believed that it lasted for six days—for three days the fair was held somewhere near the church, possibly by the Fair House (see page 111), and for three days in the town, most probably in Market Street.

Some confusion exists over the dates of the fair, and during the past two or three centuries various authorities have claimed 4th, 24th, 25th August, 10th and 16th September as the dates on which the fair was held. Of late years 16th September seems to have been accepted as the definitive date and as late as 1898 the *West Somerset Free Press* published the following in their issue of 24th September : ' On Friday last, September 16th, the juvenile element of Watchet kept the memory of Watchet fair green by promenading the streets carrying lanterns of every description and generally amusing themselves. There was a single sweet stall in Market-st., the proprietress of which had attended Watchet for many years on this date.' The custom was continued for some years and was known as ' Lantern Night'. The writer has vivid memories of taking part in one or two of these processions, around 1908–10, when the predominating type of lantern was made from a hollowed mangold in which a lighted candle was placed. The custom appears to have lapsed in more recent years.

It is possible that there were two quite distinct fairs. Several authorities claim that St. Decuman's Fair was held on either 24th or 25th August, and that Watchet Fair was held on 10th or the 16th September. At the moment there is no definite evidence by which we can establish the correct date, although we have some proof of the fair's existence down to the early part of the nineteenth century, for an entry in the churchwardens' accounts of St. Decuman's of 1821 reads : ' Mr. Leigh's [Robert Leigh, Solicitor, of Bardon] Bill for money paid by him to Mr. Marcott for advertising the discontinuance of St. Decuman's Fair in the year 1819, 24s. 5d'.

Caturn's Night

An interesting local custom which was celebrated annually on the 25th November was ' Caturn's Night'. The date was marked in Watchet and Williton, and possibly in other villages around, by the consumption of generous quantities of hot cakes and cider. The celebration usually took place in the evening, amid general merriment, to the repeated ritual of :

> ' Tis Caturn's Night I do believe
> To-morrow month be Christmas Eve'.

One of the last occasions on which this night was really celebrated was just before the great gale which destroyed the harbour in the winter of 1901. Members of the Town Band made a point of keeping up the old custom ; at the time they had a band-room above the slipway in West Street. On this particular occasion they enjoyed themselves to the full, someone having well ' laced ' the cider with whisky and rum. There was great hilarity while the party was in progress, though the story goes that several of the company were not as fresh as usual the following morning. This was indeed the last party held in the old band-room, for a few days later it was completely washed away by the terrific seas.

The origin of this custom is rather obscure ; the Watchet version appears to be as follows. A Queen Catherine, visiting Watchet when cloth-making was an important local industry, entered an establishment to watch its manufacture and is said to have called for hot cakes and cider for the workers. The Williton version, on the other hand, suggests that the feast was held in honour of St. Catherine, who was the patron saint of glovers, and that as gloving was once a local industry it was held to commemorate the saint. Here, as in the case of many local traditions and customs, we have more than one explanation, either of which may have some measure of truth.

Paper-Making

The manufacture of paper at the Watchet Paper Mills has probably been continuous for at least two centuries ; prior to this, paper-making seems to have been a very small-scale industry from the Middle Ages onwards. A great deal of the paper was made, apparently, by farmers, who no doubt found it a profitable source of income during the winter months. There is some evidence that the Watchet mill originated in this way, and was in all probability operated by the tenant farmer at Snailholt Farm, which adjoins the present mills. Another small mill of the same type in this district is mentioned in the Excise Letter of 1816. It records that William Wood was the paper-maker in charge of Egrove Mill (Williton) ; this mill, which made paper and pasteboard, changed hands after that date and in 1841 it was owned by Robert Pole. Paper-making ceased at Egrove in the year 1847 when, according to report, the proprietor was drowned in the River Parrett on returning from a trade journey to South Wales.

The present-day mill at Watchet appears to have been founded about 1750 by William Wood, who died in 1802. He was succeeded by two sons, the younger of whom, William, was in turn succeeded by his son Isaac. The Wood family held the mill until the year 1846, when it was taken over by John Wansbrough, William Peach, and James

Date. By 1869 the firm's title had become Wansbrough
and Strange, and in 1893 it was again changed to Wansbrough and Worrall. In 1896 it was formed into a public
company. There was a disastrous fire at the mill in 1898,
and (presumably as a result of the fire) a Receiver was
appointed in 1901 who controlled the mill until 1903, when
it was taken over by Mr. W. H. Reed. The writer has in
his possession a copy of a photograph of the mill taken
before the railway was extended to Minehead, in which the
mill is a very small collection of buildings clustered around
a chimney-stack which rises from the level of the meadow
beside the river. There are no buildings on the slope to
St. Decuman's Church, and it appears that the whole area
of the mill at that time hardly covered as much ground as
one of the large modern buildings which to-day stand on
the same site.

Flour-Milling

Milling was an important local industry in Watchet from
Saxon times until the early years of the present century ;
and as we saw earlier a mill was already established at the
time of the Domesday survey, where it is recorded that
it had been held by Alwold. The old Manor Mill was
certainly of ancient origin, although it is impossible to say
if its site was also that of the original Saxon mill. At least,
we know that up to the middle of the last century old
manorial customs were still obligatory to the occupier of
this mill. Three pairs of stones were worked by a water-
wheel, and during harvest the local people would bring
their gleanings to be ground, the miller being paid the cost
of grinding either in kind or in money.

There was another water-driven mill on the site of
the present Exmoor Paper and Bag Company's works. It
was much larger than the Manor Mill, having ten pairs of
stones which were kept busy day and night. In 1832 this

mill was leased to Thomas Stoate, the founder of the present flour milling firm of Stoate & Sons, Ltd., of Bristol. Some measure of its importance can be obtained from a letter written by Thomas Stoate on 21st May, 1836, in which he states that he is paying a rental of £160 per annum for the mill and twenty-one acres of land, a quite considerable amount at that time. The Manor Mill was subsequently acquired by the Stoates and the larger mill was rebuilt in 1885, new and up-to-date machinery being installed, with a steam engine and a water turbine to augment the previous water-wheels, which were inadequate to drive the new plant.

The Iron-Ore Mines and The West Somerset Mineral Railway.

The Ebbw Vale Iron and Steel Company opened iron-ore mines on the Brendon Hills in the year 1852, and at the same time the West Somerset Mineral Railway was constructed to transport the ore to Watchet, whence it was shipped to the iron works of South Wales. The railway ran from Watchet harbour to the foot of the Brendon Hills at Combe Row, and from this point the trucks were hauled up a very steep incline by means of stationary winding gear housed at the summit. The development of the mines and the railway was of the greatest importance to Watchet harbour, and we read that ' in July 1860 eleven ships left Watchet in one week loaded with ore.' From 1873 to 1878 the average figure for the export of ore from Watchet to South Wales was over 40,000 tons a year ; unfortunately, the low quality of the ore mined made the project uneconomic, and in the year 1899 both the mines and the railway were closed.

In September, 1865, a passenger service was opened on the railway between Watchet and Combe Row ; the formal opening, according to the *West Somerset Free Press* of 9th September of that year, was a most important event for the district. At 11 o'clock the train, crowded with excited

passengers and pulled by the engine ' Rowcliffe', which was
decorated with flowers, left the station at Watchet (i.e.,
the Mineral Railway Station at the end of Market Street)
to the deafening roar of many cannons. At Washford and
Roadwater the stations were gaily decorated with flowers
and flags and were crowded with passengers, who piled into
the train for the last lap to Combe Row. There the crowd,
later swollen by further train-loads from Watchet, ' engaged
in an alfresco meal—and in various amusements, the Watchet
Fife and Drum Band also being present.'

Three classes were provided for the passengers, and
some examples of the fares charged are as follows :

Watchet to Washford :
First 4d.   Second 3d.   Third 2d. Single Fare.
Watchet to Roadwater :
First 8d.   Second 6d.   Third 4d.   ,,   ,,
Watchet to Combe Row :
First 1/-. Second 9d.   Third 6d.   ,,   ,,

The Railway to Taunton
The first half of the nineteenth century was a time of
great railway activity throughout the country, and among
the hundreds of schemes put forward there were several
affecting the West Country.   The first project concerning
Watchet was ' The Bristol and English Channel Direct
Junction Railway ', which was given a prominent advertisement in the *Taunton Courier* of 27th August, 1845.   The
railway, which was to run from Watchet to Bridport, required a capital of £500,000.   The advantages claimed for
this line were that it would avoid the ' tedius, dangerous
and very circuitous passage of the Land's End '.   It was
also claimed that Wales and Ireland would be brought nearer
to London by 200 to 300 miles.   A later advertisement
stated that Watchet was the most important port on the

English side of the Bristol Channel. Locally, there was considerable support for the scheme and a good deal of preliminary surveying was done, but, like many other railway projects of the period, it was eventually abandoned.

The following year another scheme was put forward to link Bridgwater to Minehead, through Watchet; this also fell through at the time, only to be revived in the year 1882 as the Bridgwater to Watchet Railway. The proposed route was from Bridgwater through Cannington, Nether Stowey, Stogursey, Kilve, East Quantoxhead, St. Audries (where a short tunnel was to be cut), to Doniford, where the line would join the existing railway. Again there appears to have been a good deal of local backing for this scheme, which needed a capital of £360,000. The necessary Bill was presented to the House of Commons and in due course received the Royal Assent, but apparently the required capital was not subscribed, so this project, like its predecessors, did not materialize.

With the reconstruction of the harbour and the general increase in trade, the need for better and more modern methods of transport was met by the extension of the railway to Watchet in the year 1862. The West Somerset Company, which was to bring the line from the Bristol and Exeter Company's line, near Taunton, to Watchet, was incorporated in 1857, under the chairmanship of Sir Peregrine Acland. Great difficulty was encountered in raising sufficient capital for the project, and it was not until the 10th April, 1859, that work was started at Crowcombe Heathfield. The original engineer was Brunel, though he apparently handed over to his assistant Brereton in the early stages of the work. The line was a creditable feat of engineering for those times; the difficult country through which the track had to be built meant many high banks and deep cuttings, as well as severe curves and steep gradients. When completed the line was leased to the Bristol and Exeter Company and opened for passenger traffic on the 31st March, 1862.

The formal opening of the railway was, according to the *West Somerset Free Press* of 5th April, 1862, a most memorable occasion. The Band of the 26th Somerset Carriage Shed Rifle Corps played through the town, which was gaily decorated with arches and garlands. At the Station entrance was a triumphal arch with the motto, ' Welcome, ye friends of Progress', and among other mottoes was ' Welcome to all Strangers to Watchet for by your Aid shall our Commerce develop '. The above Band was later joined on the Esplanade by the Milverton Band, and musical selections were played while a public dinner was in progress. The vicar of St. Decuman's, the Rev. Robert Poole, better known locally as Parson Poole, presided. The dinner, so the report says, was ' of a most sumptuous and récherché character'; many toasts were drunk to the promotors of the railway and to the town and trade of Watchet.

The Minehead Railway Company was formed to extend the line to Minehead in 1865 ; this company, however, failed to proceed with the work and was dissolved in 1870. In the following year the company was reformed and work proceeded, the extension from Watchet to Minehead being opened on 16th July, 1874. The extension was also worked by the Bristol and Exeter Company, which used and maintained the lines for an annual rent. It is interesting to note that the Minehead Company was taken over in 1897 by the Great Western Railway, which company had already amalgamated with the Bristol and Exeter Company in 1896. The West Somerset Company survived until 1922, when it was absorbed by the Great Western under the compulsory grouping of the railways into four companies.

PLATE XIII

THE 'QUEEN BEE', THE FIRST RADIO-CONTROLLED 'PLANE, ON THE LAUNCHING
RAMP AT DONIFORD IN THE LATE 1930s.

PLATE XIV

RUSSIAN FREIGHTER IN WATCHET HARBOUR, NOVEMBER, 1972

The End of the Nineteenth Century

The later part of the nineteenth century meant busy days for Watchet. The harbour was invariably a centre of great activity, for shipments of timber, paper, iron-ore, flour and other merchandise kept the fleet of vessels and the two railways constantly on the move. Watchet also possessed several small workshops which employed quite a number of people between them. At The Cross was a saw-mill owned by Mr. R. J. Thorne, and on the corner of Goviers Lane and the Doniford Road was another small mill operated by Mr. John Ennis.

In Swain Street there was a busy foundry owned by Messrs. J. Gliddon and Son, of Williton, where many types of engineering were carried on. Every week the foundry furnaces glowed and the molten metal, poured into moulds, came out a few days later as castings for the machines of the paper-mills, the iron-ore mines, and the various works and mills of the district. Another engineering establishment at Mount Pleasant was owned by Messrs. J. Chidgey and Sons ; this firm specialized in water-wheels and turbines, as well as brass-moulding. Many of the water-wheels and turbines in the surrounding district, some of which may be still found working, were made and assembled here.

A minor industry which continued until well into the present century was that of ropemaking. It was another family business and was last worked by the late Mr. John Besley and his sons. The earliest ropewalk site was situated somewhere between Swain Street and Station Road, but the business was moved, probably about a century and a half ago, to a site near The Cross. The tithe map of 1841 shows a small building on the road near the lower entrance to the present Community Centre, which is referred to in the Tithe Apportionments List as the Wheel House or Ropewalk, and the ropes were made on a strip of land at the side of the road. With the coming of the railway this building and others adjacent were pulled down to make room for the station buildings, and the Ropewalk was removed to the Doniford Road, where ropes were still made until the nineteen-twenties.

The Besley family were well-known fishermen and were famed for the use of the boats known as Watchet ' flatties '. These flat-bottomed and double-prowed boats, it is believed, were to be found only in the estuary of the River Parrett and in Watchet. They were built locally by rule-of-thumb methods, and were extremely useful and handy boats for fishing. It has been suggested that they were made in the traditional manner of the Viking boats, with which they have some similarities ; one very striking link is that the balers of the boats were carved from a single piece of wood and closely resemble balers excavated with Viking ships in Scandinavia.

Shipbuilding continued until the later part of the century, a well-known Watchet vessel *The Star of the West* being built in the 1850's on a site bordering Yard beach, from which she was launched. The last boat of any size to be built at Watchet was a steam yacht thirty-four feet in length. This boat, named the *Florence*, was built in 1878 and was intended for short pleasure trips ; she was capable of carrying twenty passengers. The builder, Benjamin Williams, was apparently a very competent boat-builder, for in 1870 he built the *Periton*, a sailing ship of seventy-nine tons at Minehead.

Ship repairs also continued into the present century ; quite often the late Mr. N. Besley and Mr. W. Jones, with helpers, could be seen trimming a new mast on the east wharf, or at their workshop in the Esplanade Road ; at other times they could be seen caulking the seams of one of the old vessels, high and dry between the tides, in the harbour mouth. These are sights we shall see no more, for not only are the old craftsmen gone but the ships in which they took so much pride also belong to the past.

During this period Watchet appears to have steadily progressed ; the town was lit by gas early in the year 1867, and a company was formed in 1889 to supply the town with piped water. Previously the people of Watchet relied on wells for their water supply, but with the development of building and industry the need for a modern method of supply was the subject of much local agitation.

At a meeting of Watchet ratepayers held in February, 1885, Mr. W. L. Copp reported that the committee appointed at the previous meeting had inspected places in the town which required water. They recommended the sinking of five new wells and the deepening of several others. It was mentioned that seven of the town's wells became brackish and unfit to drink on every high tide. It was said that the chief part of the town depended for its supply on a tank in the Mineral Railway yard, which was fed from the Brendon Hills. Objections were raised when it was suggested that a supply be brought from Washford to Watchet at an approximate cost of £1,000, and the committee's recommendations were agreed to.

In January of the following year, 1886, the *West Somerset Free Press* carried the following report : ' Analysis of samples from eight of Watchet's sixty-two wells were submitted at the adjourned Local Government Board inquiry held there in respect of an application by Williton Sanitary Authority for the constitution of a special drainage district to comprise the town of Watchet for the purpose of providing a water supply. The samples showed all the water in the eight wells to be unfit for drinking purposes, and the inspector said it was clearly the duty of the Sanitary Authority to provide the town with a proper supply. After getting his report he thought the Local Government Board would no doubt call on them to prepare a scheme.'

So the nineteenth century drew to a close, with the people of Watchet still living in a fairly compact little community centred around the old town and the harbour, as it must have been since Saxon times.

A great deal of the social life of the town was centred around the different churches, while at outside events such as sports, fêtes, the annual regatta, and so on, the Town Band was in demand. There appear to have been four bands in Watchet from the middle of the nineteenth century. The Paper Mill's Band, the St. Decuman's Band, and towards the end of the century the D Company Volunteer Band of the Territorials, from which ultimately came the present Watchet Town Band.

On rare occasions the town was visited by travelling theatrical companies who played ' Maria Marten ' and other popular dramas of the period in a large room at the West Somerset Hotel. Other popular entertainments were the periodic visits of the Walford Family, a company of travelling entertainers whose programmes of songs, dances, and lantern shows were always appreciated. The writer believes it was this company that first showed ' motion pictures ' in Watchet early in the present century. On the whole people made their own amusement, and local concerts were ever-popular events.

The beginning of the new century brought the greatest material disaster in Watchet's long history. On the night of the twenty-eighth of December, 1901, as a result of a tremendous gale, combined with an exceptionally high tide, a large portion of the harbour was washed away and many ships lying inside were wrecked or badly damaged, the resulting loss to the town being estimated at over £20,000.

The calamity, far from bringing Watchet's history to a close, appears to have roused the progressive section of the townsfolk into great activity. Meetings were convened and much discussion took place as to the future of the harbour and the town, the outcome of which was the formation of an urban district council; capital was borrowed on the security of the port revenue and the general rates, and the harbour undertaking was taken over by the newly-formed council from the Harbour Commissioners. The work of rebuilding was commenced, chiefly on the western side where the damage had been greatest, the result being the fine and not inartistic breakwater that we see to-day.

The increase of the population has been practically continuous since 1900, as the following figures show : 1902, 1,887 ; 1921, 1,814 ; 1939, 2,244 ; 1951, 2,600. The higher figure given for 1902 was due to the large number of outside workers engaged in rebuilding the harbour. The town's expansion is even more marked by the rate of building. At the beginning of the present century the south side of the town consisted chiefly of Sea View, Almyr, Portland, Gladstone, Causeway, and Wristland Terraces, with a few older houses at Mount Pleasant, the cottages on the Doniford Road, known as New Buildings, and a few odd houses such as Temple Villas, Wristland, etc., while Malvern Road, Severn and Gillham Terraces were in course of erection. Since then over two hundred and fifty houses have been built on the south side of the town alone.

The paper mills have steadily expanded their production, continually adding new buildings and introducing new machinery. A century ago the mill buildings could scarcely have covered an acre of ground, whereas to-day they cover five to six times such an area. In the year 1910 an innovation in Watchet's trade was the import of wood-pulp direct from Scandinavia for paper making, a trade

that has constantly increased, with the exception of the
two war periods, until the present time, when the annual
imports of wood-pulp average about 25,000 tons. Esparto
grass from North Africa is also imported in substantial
quantities, and although it is not used at the Watchet mills
(being conveyed by rail to other mills connected with the
Wansbrough Paper Company) it brings considerable revenue
to the harbour.

The flour mills of Stoate and Sons were another source
of business activity in the early part of the century, employing a number of people in the mills as well as being responsible
for a great deal of harbour traffic. This included the import
of wheat and coal and the export of flour to South Wales,
Bristol, and Ireland. In the year 1911 a disastrous fire
at the larger mill practically destroyed the plant. The
directors decided not to rebuild but to move the business
to Bristol, where a more modern and up-to-date mill was
in course of erection. At the same time it was decided to
discontinue milling at the old manor mill. The closing down
of the two mills brought to an end an industry that had
been continuous in Watchet for over a thousand years.
The derelict mill was taken over and rebuilt in 1916 by the
Exmoor Paper and Bag Company, who had purchased the
paper-bag plant and business formerly operated by the
Wansbrough Paper Company. To-day paper bags of all
types are manufactured by this firm and sent to all parts
of the country.

In 1908 the attempt made to open the iron-ore mines
on the Brendon Hills again brought into use the Mineral
Railway. Ore to the value of £18,000 was mined and shipped
from Watchet to South Wales; unfortunately the venture
proved to be uneconomic, chiefly owing to the large quantities
of cheaper iron-ore then arriving from Spain, and the mines
and railway were finally closed for this purpose in 1909.

The railway was again used for a short period in 1911–1912 by an engineering company for the experimental work on an electrical braking system. During the 1914–18 war the permanent way was dismantled and removed to other parts of the country, and all that now remains of the ' Mineral Railway', as it is known locally, is the narrow, and now much-overgrown strip of land, winding up to the foot of the Brendon Hills at Combe Row.

The First World War took a heavy toll of Watchet men in proportion to the population, no less than thirty-seven men losing their lives on land and sea. Many of Watchet's ships and sailors were also involved in the carrying of stores and equipment to France ; most of the ships went in guarded convoys, but occasionally a local captain would risk a solo trip, more than one of which brought some exciting adventures to the captain and crew. While the town received a few evacuees as a result of Zeppelin raids on London, as well as two or three refugee families from Belgium, the effect of the war was almost unnoticeable compared with that of the 1939–45 war. Within a few days of the latter's outbreak in September, 1939, the population was almost doubled as a result of the evacuation of London and the larger cities and towns ; this influx of people was further increased by the addition of large numbers of service personnel at the nearby camps. With the complete blackout, and the heavy air raids on Swansea, Cardiff, Bristol, and Weston, when enemy bombers flying over Watchet to these targets occasionally dropped a stick of bombs if hard pressed by fighter planes, conditions in Watchet were totally different from those of 1914–18. While the death-roll of Watchet men were not so high as in the earlier war, it is tragic to record that sixteen men were killed on active service.

In 1920 an attempt was made to set up a shipbreaking yard. A part of the West Pier and adjoining yards were leased by the Cardiff Shipbreaking Company, and the former flagship of the Pacific fleet, *H.M.S. Fox*, a cruiser of 6,000 tons, was brought into the harbour and broken up. The company discontinued work at Watchet in 1922 and, although another firm took over the site for a period, difficulties created by the post-war slump made it impossible for work to continue at Watchet, and the venture ended in 1923.

Considerable changes, many almost imperceptible, have occurred over the past fifty years. The foundries in Swain Street and Mount Pleasant have been closed these many years, as also have been the timber yards at The Cross and Doniford Road. Other minor industries originating many centuries ago, lime-burning, fishing, rope-making, cloth-making, and tanning, have all ceased. Mechanical progress has been most marked for those of us who remember the past half century; the author remembers seeing, when a boy, the first motor-car in Watchet, and the first aeroplane to fly over the town. At that time there were between sixty to seventy horses kept in Watchet—to-day there is only one. During the same period the number of motor vehicles has increased until they far exceed the number of horses of fifty years ago.

During the past half century Watchet can claim to have made substantial material progress. Immediately after the First World War the urban council embarked on their first housing project at Flowerdale, the first of a series which, though interrupted during 1939–1945, continues. From 1918 to 1939 seventy-six council houses were erected, while in the eight years since the end of the Second World War over one hundred houses have been completed.

Opportunities for improvement have not been neglected by the local council and the townspeople, as can be seen by noting the town's amenities. Watchet is justly proud of its delightful Memorial Ground. Conceived as a memorial to the fallen of the 1914–1918 war, it is situated on the old strip cultivations known in the past as Culvercliff; here, surrounded by a grand panorama of hills, stretching from the Quantocks to the heart of Exmoor, is a fitting tribute to the men of a community who have long been proud of their sportsmanship at football and cricket.

After the last war the British Restaurant was purchased by the urban council on behalf of the townspeople and later converted into a Community Centre. A committee, representative of all the churches and secular bodies in the town then took over from the council, raised funds by public subscription, and obtained grants from various bodies, the council were repaid, the committee accepting full responsibility of management. The Centre is used for innumerable functions by practically every organization in the town, and is generally acclaimed as a great acquisition. When we consider the endless memorials throughout the country, many of which can only be described as sculptural monstrosities, we can be grateful for the originality and practical common sense of those who sponsored these schemes.

A cultural asset, due to the generosity of a former inhabitant, Mr. Leonard Stoate, was the opening of a Public Library in May, 1953. The old disused Lifeboat House was converted and modernized; now with a stock of 5,000 volumes, ranging from a children's section to fiction, history, travel, and reference works, it is an institution greatly appreciated by readers both young and old.

Summer visitors still find charm in Watchet and the surrounding countryside; in addition to the large number who stay in the town, many hundreds visit the holiday camps at Helwell Bay, West Bay, and Warren Farm. The increase in road travel, by bus, coach, and motor-car, enables the visitor to-day to see much more of the beauty of West

Somerset than formerly. It has also created greater opportunities for the inhabitants to know and appreciate the lovely surroundings in which they live. With the telephone, the cinema, wireless, and now television, the people of Watchet, with other country districts, have completely lost that isolation due to their geographical position which was the lot of their ancestors.

The old order has passed and a new takes its place; this too, in turn, will give way to fresh social and material changes, but withal we feel confident that the people of Watchet, like their forefathers before them, will meet their responsibilities and problems with courage and foresight, and like them will triumph over future difficulties.

We end our history from the same vantage point as we began, overlooking our ancient harbour, the scene over the centuries of so much anxiety and hope for the people of Watchet. Now where the old wooden ships of Watchet traded for so many centuries come modern steam and motor ships from British, Continental, and Scandinavian ports. It is here that we see real human progress; whereas the first ships from Scandinavia, manned by the warlike Viking raiders, entered the harbour over a thousand years ago bent on ' much evil and manslaying ', their descendants now bring the raw material on which the livelihood of a large part of our population depends; thus the raiders of the past have become the friendly traders of the present.

POSTSCRIPT 1973

Eighteen years have passed since this history was first published, years in which changes have taken place in many directions. Changes too, which would have bewildered our forefathers with their speed, for to them living in a more leisurely age change was a far more gradual process.

The tremendous increase in motor traffic for instance, has compelled the Urban District Council to make two sizeable car parks, in which visitors and shoppers can leave their cars in comparative safety, as well as preventing congestion in our narrow streets—streets which, after all, were only visualised for horse traffic. In order to make the first of these it was necessary to pull down a large part of the building in Swain Street, formerly Snell's Bakery, and more recently known as Saskatoon Cafe. The other car park, adjoining the Bell Inn, in Market Street, meant the destruction of several old cottages; in one of these a plaster plaque, on the bedroom wall, bore the inscription T N. D N. H. N. 1630. Although we have no record of the family who lived there at that time, two old families, the Nicholas's, or Norman's, might well have been the original occupants.

Despite the fact that a few old cottages have been demolished, new building has gone forward at a steady pace. During the past eighteen years the Urban District Council have built a considerable number of houses at Reed Close, and on land adjoining Woodland Road. Nearby, the War Department also built a number of houses for military personnel stationed at Doniford Camp. Private building has also been responsible for the erection of further houses. The following figures show that Watchet has an excellent record for housing. In 1955 there were 851 dwellings in the Urban District, today, 1973, there are 1,148, an increase of 297 houses during the period under review.

The greatest development in Watchet during the past few years has been the revival of the harbour trade. After the war the chief imports were wood-pulp, esparto grass, and coal, all of which was used by the local Paper Mills, and other mills of the group at Silverton and Cullompton in Devon. When the local Mills changed over from coal to oil burning, imports of coal were discontinued, and as a result, both tonnage and dues from the harbour were affected. In 1967–8 negotiations took place between the Urban District Council and some shipping companies for port facilities, and a steady build-up of harbour trade began to develop. Today there are two shipping companies engaged in regular import and export of goods, and the harbour is now the scene of almost continuous activity.

The firm of Chas. M. Willie & Co., Shipping Ltd., have a regular fleet on charter, sailing from Portugal to Watchet; they include the s.s. *Watchet Star, North Star, East Star, Douro Star,* and the *Aveiro Star*. These boats bring in wine, corks, bulk-cork, box-wood, hardboard, chip-board, linen, children's clothing, glassware, animal feeding stuff, wire-coils, steel-rods, and paper, all imported from Portugal.

Considerable quantities of timber are also imported in other ships from Sweden and the U.S.S.R., while occasional ships from Spain and Italy bring cargoes of fruit-pulp, canned tomatoes, tomato-puree, fruit salad, apricots and other goods.

Whereas the boats which in the past brought wood-pulp and esparto grass to Watchet left without cargo to other ports, the boats now load export cargo from Watchet, chiefly to Portugal, one of the chief exports being crated motor car parts, from the British Leyland Group, to an assembly plant at

Setubal in Portugal. Other exports include zinc, sheet steel, powdered aluminium, waste paper, rubber, and cardboard. An interesting export in the early part of 1972 was a complete prefabricated hotel, which was shipped direct to Gibraltar. The Bristol and Western Shipping Company, which has recently started operating here, also imports timber, tea and other merchandise.

The wharf has been greatly extended as a result of the railway closure, the former goods sidings having been taken up and the whole area devoted to harbour traffic, and storage space. A large warehouse has also been built on the east wharf, and at the time of writing another warehouse, for the Bristol and Western Shipping Company, is in the early stages of erection near the railway crossing. Some idea of the value of the harbour imports and exports can be gathered from the following figures:

	Tonnage of Ships	Dues on Shipping	Tonnage of goods	Harbour Dues
1955/6	22,917	£451	50,372	£2,285
1971/2	28,248	£2,825	44,213	£6,446

Despite the fact that there is not a great deal of difference in the overall tonnage through the harbour, the greater diversity of merchandise, coupled with the export trade, has more than trebled the harbour income.

An addition to local industry has been the establishment of Protective Papers Ltd., a subsidiary of the Reed and Smith group, at the Paper Mills. This company specialises in paper converting processes, employing over a hundred workers making a wide range of paper products, including wallpapers, Christmas wrappings, ice cream wrappings, wax papers and industrial crepe papers.

The British Van Heusen Company Ltd., established over twenty years ago in premises converted from the old Cosy Cinema at The Cross, have expanded their factory and increased their production during the past few years. Over 130 operatives, the majority women, make the well known Van Heusen shirts. Exports, which amount to around 18% of their output, are sent to Zambia, Malaysia, Uganda, Kenya, and many other countries. The company have mills in the Manchester area where materials are manufactured for their factories, other materials are imported from Switzerland, Holland, Spain, and other European countries.

To many townsfolk a matter of deep regret was the failure of the Community Centre. Here was a central building suitable for public meetings, dramatics, concerts, dances, and other events which today it is often difficult to arrange for lack of suitable accommodation. Despite the enthusiasm of the committee, who made great efforts to keep it in being, it proved uneconomic, was taken over by the Urban District Council and eventually sold and converted into a garage.

A more regrettable event during this period was the closure of the Taunton to Minehead branch line. For over a century the familiar sound of the steam train, and more recently the diesel locomotive, had been heard running in and out of Watchet Station. Under the Beeching plan the line was finally closed in January 1970. At the time of writing there are great hopes of the line's revival by a private company, the West Somerset Railway Company, who aim to re-open the line from Taunton to Minehead, with both steam and diesel trains in 1973. Most local people, especially the railway enthusiasts, wish the company success and look forward eagerly to the re-opening of the line and hearing once more the familiar sound of the trains.

A closure of another kind during this period was that of the military camp at Doniford. Opened as far back as the

1920s as a summer camp for Territorials, it was later enlarged as an Anti-Aircraft Training School. During that time an experimental unit caused a great deal of interest when small, remotely controlled planes, known as "Queen Bees", were used for target practice. There were always plenty of spectators to see the "Queen Bees" launched from the catapult.

A great asset to the town was the erection of the new Red Cross centre on the Esplanade. For years the members had been housed in a hut near the harbour, often inaccessible during bad weather. Great efforts to raise funds by the members, helped by the generosity of Mrs. John Stoate, a former commandant, made it possible for the new centre to be built, and it was formally opened by Lady Wraxall in 1964. The centre has a hall, kitchen, and lecture room, which is used for training V.A.Ds and cadets. A weekly Luncheon Club is also run at the centre, which provides a midday meal, at a modest price, for about 40 elderly people, who are brought in by volunteers in their cars. Medical loans of invalid chairs, and other equipment, are also made by the organisation.

Another amenity is the Youth Club, a modern building sited on the eastern end of the Memorial Ground. This provides facilities for both juniors and seniors in the form of indoor games, dancing, and other activities.

So Watchet, our little West Somerset town with over a thousand years of history behind it, still keeps abreast of the times. That it may long continue as a friendly, close-knit community, is the earnest wish of the writer.

THE END

BIBLIOGRAPHY

(Books and Authors as referred to in the text)

Anglo-Saxon Chronicle.
ANON., *The Life of Sir Robert Blake.*
BARNARD, Dr. F. P., *Medieval England.*
BRAGG, WM., *General Directory for the County of Somerset.*
BURROUGH, E., *Camps of Somerset.*
CAMDEN, *Magna Britannia, Vol. I,* 1753.
CHADWICK-HEALEY, *History of Part of West Somerset,* 1901.
CHEYNEY, F. P., *Industrial and Social History of England.*
COLLINSON, Rev. J., *History and Antiquities of Somerset,* 1791.
COULTON, G. G., *The Medieval Village.*
DEFOE, DANIEL, *A Tour through the Island of Great Britain.*
DOBSON, D. P., *The Archaeology of Somerset.*
EELES, Dr. F. C., *St. Decuman's.*
EKWALL, E., *Concise Oxford Dictionary of English Place Names.*
EYTON, Rev. R. W., *Domesday Studies of Somerset.*
GRAY, H. St. GEORGE, *Report of Battlegore Excavation,* P.S.A.S., 1932.
GREEN, E., *Somerset and the Armada.*
GREEN, J. R., *A Short History of the English People.*
GREENWOOD, C. and J., *Somerset.*
GRESWELL, Rev. W. H. P., *The Land of Quantock.*
HAMMOND, J. L. and B., *The Village Labourer.*
HANCOCK, Preb. H., *History of Minehead.*
HILL, J. S., *The Place Names of Somerset.*
LELAND, JOHN, *Itineraries.*
MACDERMOT, E. T., *History of the Great Western Railway.*
MAJOR, ALBANY S., *Early Wars of Wessex.*
MORTON, A. L., *A Peoples History of England.*
NORTH, F. J., *The Evolution of the Bristol Channel.*
OMAN, SIR CHARLES, *England Before the Conquest.*
PAGE, J. L. W., *An Exploration of Exmoor.*
Piggotts Directory 1830.
SAVAGE, V., *The History of the Hundred of Carhampton.*
Somerset Archaeological Society. Proceedings.
Somerset and Dorset Notes and Queries. Publications.
Somerset Record Society. Publications.
STENTON, F. M., *Anglo-Saxon England.*
SYMONS, W., *Early Methodism in West Somerset.*
TREVELYAN, G. M., *English Social History.*
Universal British Directory of Trade, Commerce and Manufacture, 1794.
Victoria County History of Somerset, Vols. I and II.
WEDLAKE, A. L., *The Watchet Mint.* P.S.A.S. 1948-49.
WORSAAE, J. J. A., *The Danes and Norwegians in England, Scotland, and Ireland.*
YOUNG, A., *Annals of Agriculture.*

INDEX